前言 *PREFACE*

英国思想家培根说过：阅读使人深刻。阅读的真正目的是获取信息，开拓视野和陶冶情操。从语言学习的角度来说，学习语言若没有大量阅读就如隔靴搔痒，因为阅读中的语言是最丰富、最灵活、最具表现力、最符合生活情景的，同时读物中的情节、故事引人入胜，进而能充分调动读者的阅读兴趣，培养读者的文学修养，至此，语言的学习水到渠成。

"麦格希中英双语阅读文库"在世界范围内选材，涉及科普、社会文化、文学名著、传奇故事、成长励志等多个系列，充分满足英语学习者课外阅读之所需，在阅读中学习英语、提高能力。

◎难度适中

本套图书充分照顾读者的英语学习阶段和水平，从读者的阅读兴趣出发，以难易适中的英语语言为立足点，选材精心、编排合理。

◎精品荟萃

本套图书注重经典阅读与实用阅读并举。既包含国内外脍炙人口、耳熟能详的美文，又包含科普、人文、故事、励志类等多学科的精彩文章。

◎功能实用

本套图书充分体现了双语阅读的功能和优势，充分考虑到读者课外阅读的方便，超出核心词表的词汇均出现在使其意义明显的语境之中，并标注释义。

鉴于编者水平有限，凡不周之处，谬误之处，皆欢迎批评教正。

我们真心地希望本套图书承载的文化知识和英语阅读的策略对提高读者的英语著作欣赏水平和英语运用能力有所裨益。

丛书编委会

科学普及系列

麦格希 **中英双语阅读文库**

水是生命之源

神奇自然馆 第1辑

麦格希中英双语阅读文库编委会●编

吉林出版集团股份有限公司

图书在版编目（CIP）数据

神奇自然馆. 第1辑. 水是生命之源 / 麦格劳－
希尔教育集团主编；刘庆双，李进彪译；麦格希中英双
语阅读文库编委会编. -- 2版. -- 长春：吉林出版集团
股份有限公司, 2018.3
（麦格希中英双语阅读文库）
书名原文：Timed Readings Plus in Science Book 1
ISBN 978-7-5581-4802-6

Ⅰ. ①神… Ⅱ. ①美… ②刘… ③李… ④麦… Ⅲ.
①英语－汉语－对照读物②自然科学－普及读物 Ⅳ.
①H319.4：N

中国版本图书馆CIP数据核字(2018)第045978号

神奇自然馆　第1辑　水是生命之源

编：麦格希中英双语阅读文库编委会
插　　画：齐　航　李延霞
责任编辑：欧阳鹏
封面设计：冯冯翼
开　　本：660mm × 960mm　1/16
字　　数：225千字
印　　张：10
版　　次：2018年3月第2版
印　　次：2018年3月第1次印刷

出　　版：吉林出版集团股份有限公司
发　　行：吉林出版集团外语教育有限公司
地　　址：长春市泰来街1825号
　　　　　邮编：130011
电　　话：总编办：0431-86012683
　　　　　发行部：0431-86012767　0431-86012826(Fax)
印　　刷：香河利华文化发展有限公司

ISBN 978-7-5581-4802-6　　定价：29.90元

Contents

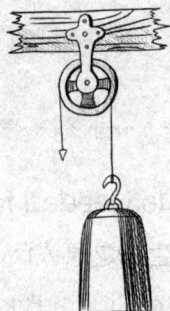

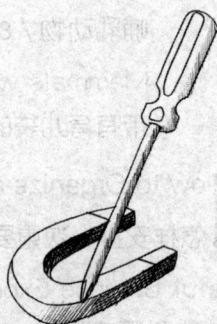

1

Water Is Needed for Life

What would happen to a *houseplant* if nobody ever watered it? It would *wilt* and die. Animals and people need water too. In fact, all living things need water to survive.

Why is water so important? It makes up most of the weight of living things. An animal's blood and the *sap* of plants are

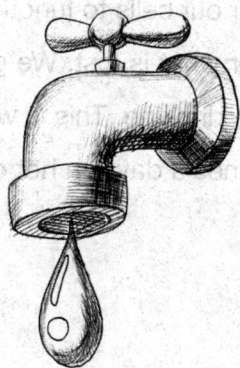

水是生命之源

盆室内的植物如果从来没有人浇水会怎么样？它会枯萎然后死掉。动物和人同样也需要水。事实上，所有的有生命的东西都需要水来生存。

水为什么这么重要？它组成了生命体的大部分。动物的血液和树的汁

---

houseplant *n.* 室内盆栽植物   wilt *v.* （使）枯萎；凋谢
sap *n.* （植物体内运送养分的）液；汁

mostly water. Blood and sap move food and get rid of waste. In the cells, chemical reactions take place. These are needed for survival, and they can't occur without water.

Our bodies lose water in many ways. We lose it through our skin when we *sweat*. We lose tiny drops of it in the air that we *exhale*. We lose it in the form of *urine*. We lose between 2 and 3 *liters* (2.1 to 3.2 quarts) of water a day. In order to keep enough water in our bodies for our cells to function, we need to take in enough water to make up for what is lost. We get some water from food, but we get most of it by drinking. This is why people need to drink a glass of water several times a day. On hot days, we sweat more, so we need to drink more.

液大部分都是水。血液和汁液运送食物并且把废物运送出去。在细胞中会发生化学反应。这些是生存所必需的，没有水，这些都不可能进行。

我们的身体会以很多种方式流失水分。当我们的皮肤出汗时会流失水分。我们呼气时会失去少量的水。水会以尿的形式流失。我们每天会流失2到3升(2.1到3.2夸脱)的水。为了使我们的身体里有足够的水保证细胞的正常工作，我们应该补充足够的水分弥补流失的那些水分。我们可以从食物中获得水，但是大部分是通过喝水获得。这就是为什么人在一天中每隔一段时间就要喝一杯水。在炎热的天气中，我们出的汗多，所以我们就要

---

sweat *v.* 出汗；流汗

urine *n.* 尿；小便

exhale *v.* 呼出；呼气

liter *n.* 公升

When the amount of water in the body falls below a certain level, we feel thirsty. Thirst is the body's way of making sure we drink what we need.

Think about the many other ways we use water each day. We use it to help us brush our teeth. We might use water to make soup for lunch. We add water to cake mixes. We give water to pets. We water the grass and the flowers in the yard. If there isn't enough rain, farmers may need to water their crops. We take a bath or shower to get clean. We use water to wash our clothes, wash the car, and *mop* the floor. We use water to put out fires.

Pure water does not have any taste or odor. But chemicals, *pesticides*, and wastes from factories have polluted our water. Water

---

喝更多的水。当我们身体中的水分含量下降到一定程度时，我们就会感觉口渴。口渴是确定我们身体需要水的一种方式。

想想我们每天用水的其他方式。我们用它来刷牙。我们也可以用它做午餐的汤。我们通过加水来调配制作蛋糕。我们给宠物喂水。我们浇园子中的花草。如果没有充足的雨水，农民需要用水来浇灌庄稼。我们用水洗澡来保持干净。我们用水洗衣服、擦车和拖地。我们用水来灭火。

纯净的水没有任何的气味。但是化学药品，杀虫剂，工厂排出的废水

---

mop *v.* 用拖把擦   pesticide *n.* 杀虫剂；除害药物

pollution can cause health problems in people and can poison *wildlife*. The water that we get from *faucets* and water *fountains* is specially cleaned to make it safe to drink. Laws have been passed to stop pollution. We need to do more to make sure that there will always be clean water for all of Earth's living things.

污染了水。水污染能引起人的健康问题并且使野生动物中毒。我们从水龙头和喷泉中得到的水是经过特殊净化的，可以安全地饮用。人们已经颁布了法律阻止污染。我们需要做更多事确保我们地球上的生物能一直使用到纯净的水。

wildlife *n.* 野生动物；野生生物　　　　　　　　faucet *n.* 龙头；旋塞
fountain *n.* 喷泉

2

Using Energy to Ride a Bike

How do the *cereal*, milk, and orange juice you had for breakfast help you ride your bike? The food that you eat is *fuel* for your body. Your body turns this fuel into energy. Your body is always making and using energy.

Just as your body is able to *transfer* energy from your stomach to your muscles,

用能量骑自行车

你早餐吃的谷类、牛奶和桔子汁怎么能帮你骑自行车？你所吃的食物都在为你的身体的提供燃料。你的身体把燃料转化成能量。你的身体在时时刻刻制造和使用能量。

就像你的身体能把胃里的能量转移到肌肉一样，来自于自行车踏板

---

cereal *n.* 谷类食物　　　　　　　　　　　　fuel *n.* 燃料
transfer *v.* 转移

a bike is able to transfer energy from its *pedals* to its wheels. The pedals are attached to a *cogwheel*, which is a wheel with metal teeth. A chain connects this cogwheel with a smaller cogwheel that is attached to the *rear* wheel. As the larger cogwheel turns, the chain makes the rear cogwheel turn the rear wheel. As the rear wheel begins to turn, the front wheel begins to turn too.

Once you get the bike started, the wheels allow it to roll easily. When one surface rolls over another, the movement causes *friction*, or resistance, which slows you down. Bike tires are narrow. There is little friction when the small surface of a bike tire rolls across the ground. Bicycle wheels are lightweight. This is because it takes

的能量能够转移到车轮。踏板和自行车的齿轮相连，齿轮是一个有金属齿的轮子。一条车链子把这个齿轮和一个与后面的车轮连着的较小的齿轮相连。当较大的齿轮转的时候，车链子会使后面的齿轮带动后轮转动。当后车轮开始转动后，前面的车轮也开始转动。

　　一旦你让自行车开始动起来，车轮会让它很容易地滚动。当一个表面滚过另一个表面，这个运动会引起摩擦，或者是阻力，这些都会让你慢下来。自行车的轮胎很窄。当自行车的轮胎很窄的表面滚过地面时，会产生小的摩擦。自行车的轮胎很轻。这是因为自行车带动轻的轮子要比带动重

---

pedal *n.* 脚蹬子；踏板
rear *adj.* 后面的；后部的

cogwheel *n.* 齿轮
friction *n.* 摩擦；摩擦力

less energy to turn a light wheel than it does to turn a heavy one. Lightweight wheels still have to be strong enough to support the weight of the bicycle and the rider. This is the reason wheels have spokes—to add strength.

Why do you have to pedal harder when going up a hill? You need more energy to overcome the force of gravity. The force of gravity increases as you go up a hill.

When you want to stop your bike, you pull the brake *levers*. These levers pull *cables* that move *pads* against the *rim* of the wheel. These pads create friction on the rim and slow the wheel down until the bike stops.

的轮子所需的能量少。轻的车轮仍然需要有足够的能量来支撑自行车和骑车人的重量。这就是为什么自行车会有车辐条——为了增加它的力量。

为什么当你上山的时候，你不得不更用力地踩脚踏板呢？你需要更多的能量去克服重力。当你上山的时候重力会增加。

当你想要停下来的时候，你要捏刹车把手。把手制动时支架上的刹车片在拉线的带动下夹紧车轮边缘从而产生制动力。车盘在轮子的边上产生摩擦力使车子减速，直到自行车停下来。

---

lever *n.* 操纵杆；控制杆　　　　　　cable *n.* 缆绳；钢索
pad *n.* 垫状物；软材料　　　　　　　rim *n.* 边沿；轮缘

Remember to wear a helmet when you ride your bike. If you fall off your bike, you may hit your head. This can cause serious damage to your brain. Most helmets have a hard shell with a layer of stiff foam. The foam can absorb most of the energy of your head's hitting the pavement. Be sure your helmet has a strong strap that will keep it on your head. When you fall off a bike, you may hit your head more than once.

So eat your breakfast, buckle on your helmet, and have a good ride!

当你骑车的时候要记得戴上头盔。如果你从自行车上掉下来，你可能会摔着你的头。这有可能会对你的大脑产生严重的损坏。大多数的头盔有很硬的壳，带有一层硬质的泡沫橡胶。泡沫橡胶能够吸收你的头部撞击地面而产生的大部分能量。一定要确保你的头盔有一个足够结实的带子能使它固定在你的头上。当你从自行车上掉下来时，可能会不只一次摔到你的头。

那么，吃早餐，扣上头盔，享受一次美好的骑车之旅！

3

Fixing a Flat

My cousin Maria and I were riding our bikes. While we rode, we talked about her problem. She didn't have a *topic* for her science project. We were *swapping* ideas when I started running out of breath. At the same time, the ride got *bumpy* and I slowed down. As Maria shot ahead of me, she said, "Didn't you eat

修理瘪胎

我和我表妹玛丽亚正在骑自行车。我们一边骑，一边讨论她的问题。她的科研项目还没有题目。当我开始喘不过气的时候，我们正在交换各自的想法。同时，自行车到了崎岖不平的地方，我慢了下来。玛丽亚骑到了我的前面，她说，"你今天早上没有吃早餐吗，佩德

---

topic *n.* 话题；题目   swap *v.* 交换
bumpy *adj.* 崎岖不平的；颠簸的

breakfast this morning, Pedro?" Maria likes to *tease* me.

When I stopped and got off my bike, I heard *hissing*. The air was *leaking* out of my back tire! There was a piece of broken glass stuck in it. "Now you're the one with a problem," Maria said. She had come back to *check on* me.

"Now I know why it was hard to ride. Remember what we learned in science class? When the tire rolls over the road, it causes friction. The more friction, the harder it is to push the wheel. As the air leaked out of my tire, it got flatter."

"So when it got flatter, there was more surface and more friction," Maria added.

罗?"玛丽亚喜欢取笑我。

当我停下来,下了自行车之后,我听到了嘶嘶声。我的自行车后轮胎漏气了!有一小块碎玻璃扎进自行车胎里了。玛丽亚说,"现在你有麻烦了。"她返回来帮我检查。

"现在我知道为什么它难骑了。还记得我们在科学课堂上学过的吗?当轮胎在路面上滚动时,它会引起摩擦。摩擦力越大,越难推动轮子前进。当轮胎漏气后,轮胎就变瘪了。"

"因此,当轮胎变瘪后,会有更大的表面积进而产生更大的摩擦力。"玛丽亚补充说。

---

tease *v.* 取笑;戏弄

leak *v.* 泄露;漏出

hiss *v.* 发嘶嘶声

check on 检查

We pushed our bikes to the gas station. I got out my patch *kit* and fixed the tire. When we got back onto our bikes, Maria said, "For my science project, I'm going to show the relationship between air pressure in a bike tire and how much of the tire touches the road."

我把自行车推到了加油站，取出了我的修理包开始修理轮胎。当我们重新骑上自行车的时候，玛丽亚说，"我的科研项目，打算解释自行车胎里的空气压力和轮胎接触地面之间的关系。"

---

kit *n.* 成套工具

4

Animals of the Forests

Forests provide *habitats*, or homes, for many animals. There are many different kinds of forests. These include *tropical* rain forests, *temperate* rain forests, and *deciduous* forests.

Tropical rain forests are hot and wet. They are hot because they are near the equator, and they are wet because it rains a lot—more than

森林里的动物

森林为许多动物提供栖息地和家。有许多不同种类的森林，包括热带雨林、温带雨林和温带落叶林。

热带雨林很热并且潮湿。那里热是因为接近赤道，潮湿是因为降雨量很大——每年有多于250厘米（100英寸）的降雨量。热带雨林里有很高

---

habitat *n.* 栖息地
temperate *adj.* 温带的

tropical *adj.* 热带的
deciduous *adj.* 落叶的

250 centimeters (100 inches) per year. Tropical rain forests have tall evergreen trees covered with vines and moss. The tallest trees are known as emergents. Eagles nest here and *swoop* down to catch a bird or a small monkey from the treetops below.

The *canopy*, or roof, of the forest is made up of the tops of the tall trees. Fruits, nuts, seeds, and leaves grow here. These things are food for many animals, including bats, parrots, and *sloths*. Some animals drink water from plants that are shaped like bowls.

Below the canopy is the understory, which is made up of bushes and the lower parts of trees. Here, monkeys with long arms swing from tree to tree. Flying squirrels and frogs glide through tree *limbs*. Snakes, birds, jaguars, and bugs also live here.

The lowest part of the rain forest is the floor. It is dark and covered

---

的常青树，它们被蔓藤和青苔覆盖着。最高的树被认为是自然生长的。鹰在这里筑巢，从树顶上俯冲下来捕捉鸟类或是小猴子。

森林的树冠或树的最高顶部是由最高树木的顶端组成的。水果、坚果、种子和叶子在这里生长。这些东西是很多动物的食物，包括蝙蝠、鹦鹉和树懒。一些动物从形状像碗的植物中饮水。

树冠下面是下层植被，它是由灌木和树的下部分组成的。在这里，长臂猴从一棵树荡到另一棵树上。鼯鼠和青蛙在树枝上滑行。蛇、鸟类、美洲虎和昆虫也生活在这里。

雨林中最低的部分是地面。这里很黑并且覆盖了很多枯萎的植物。啪

---

swoop *v.* 向下猛冲；俯冲　　canopy *n.* （尤指森林里）天蓬似的树荫；（树）冠
sloth *n.* 树懒　　　　　　　limb *n.* （树的）大枝；主枝

with dead plants. *Rodents* hide in *shrubs* here. Bigger animals, like the *tapir*, use their *snouts* to dig for roots. Thousands of kinds of insects also live in the forest.

Like tropical rain forests, temperate rain forests are wet and have tall trees. Temperate rain forests are found along the western coasts of North America and South America. They are cooler than the tropical forests, and so they have different kinds of plants and animals. Some animals, such as owls and opossums, live in the trees. Others live on the forest floor, including deer, bears, frogs, and skunks. Unlike tropical rain forests, temperate rain forests have one type of tree that is dominant in the area.

Another kind of forest is the temperate deciduous forest. These woods are drier than rain forests. The trees here do not grow as tall.

齿类动物藏在这里的灌木丛中。较大的动物，像貘用它们的鼻子去挖洞找树根。上千种的昆虫也生活在森林中。

像热带雨林一样，温带雨林也很潮湿，有许多高大的树木。温带雨林生长在北美和南美的西海岸。这里要比热带雨林温度低一些，因此这里有许多不同种类的植物和动物。一些动物，像猫头鹰，负鼠住在树上。其他的动物包括鹿、熊、蛙和臭鼬住在森林中的地面上。和热带雨林不同，温带雨林在一个区域有一种类型的树占主导地位。

另外一种森林是温带落叶林。这里的树木要比雨林中的树木干燥。这里的树长得不高。在这里也可以找到热带雨林中的一些动物。有鹿、熊

---

rodent *n.* 啮齿动物　　　　　　　shrub *n.* 灌木

tapir *n.* 貘　　　　　　　　　　snout *n.* （猪等动物的）口鼻部

Some animals that live in the temperate rain forest can be found here too. Some of these are deer, bears, and frogs. Rain forests have evergreen trees, but deciduous forests have trees that lose their leaves in the fall. The animals here may have to survive cold winters. Some *hibernate*. Some birds, such as robins, fly to a warmer place during the winter.

和蛙。雨林中有常青树，但是落叶林中的树木的叶子会在秋天掉落。这里的动物不得不在寒冷的冬天生存。一些动物选择冬眠。一些鸟类，如知更鸟，会在冬天飞到比较暖和的地方。

hibernate v. 冬眠

5

A Listening Walk in the Forest

Gram and Kevin went for a listening walk in the forest. They were quiet as they followed a narrow path through the trees. Soon they heard a long whistle, followed by "to-wit, to-wit, to-wit." High in a tree, Kevin saw a bright red bird. He pointed it out to Gram. She smiled and whispered, "That is a *cardinal*. See the red *crest* on top of its head?"

Kevin nodded, and then they went on. Suddenly they heard the

漫步在森林里聆听自然

格莱姆和凯文在森林里散步聆听自然。他们穿过静静地树林中一条窄路。很快，他们听到了一声很长的口哨声。凯文看到了一只鲜红色的鸟在树的高处。他把它指给了格莱姆。她微笑着低声说道，"那是红衣凤头鸟。看到它头顶上的红色鸟冠了吗？"

凯文点点头，然后他们继续走。突然，他们听到了树枝断裂的声音，在灌木丛中有沙沙声。三头鹿跳过小道，它们白色的尾巴像旗帜一样摆

cardinal *n.* 红衣凤头鸟　　　　　　　　　　　crest *n.* 鸟冠；羽冠

snap of a twig and a rustle in the brush. Three deer bounded across the trail, their white tails *flicking* like flags. "White-tailed deer," Gram murmured.

They continued their walk. The next sound they heard was a small *thump* near the trail. The noise came again. This time, something dropped from the air right past Kevin's nose and landed at his feet. It was a green nut with a cap on it. Kevin saw it was an acorn. He looked up and saw a squirrel run along a tree branch. "Oak tree," he whispered to Gram.

They walked on and heard a *muffled* rushing sound. The sound grew louder and louder until finally they came to a *creek* where a brown mother duck was swimming with her babies. "Mallards," they said in unison. Kevin and Gram sat down to rest on a big flat rock. Kevin wondered what they would hear on the way home.

动。格莱姆喃喃道，"白尾巴的鹿。"

他们继续走，听到的下一个声音是在小路附近轻微撞击的声音。声音又一次出现了。这时，有东西从空中掉下来，正好从凯文的鼻子边滑落在了他的脚上。它是一个绿色的坚果，上面有菌帽。凯文看到它是一个橡果。他抬头看到一只松鼠在沿着树枝跑。"是橡树，"他对格莱姆说。

他们继续走，听到了一阵模糊的哗哗声。声音变得越来越大，直到他们最终到达一条小溪旁，那里，一只棕色的鸭妈妈正在和它的孩子们游泳。"野鸭子，"他们同时说。凯文和格莱姆坐在大而扁平的岩石上休息。凯文在想他们在回家的路上会听到什么。

---

flick *v.* 轻弹；轻拍
muffled *adj.* 压抑的；模糊不清的

thump *n.* 碰撞声；重击声
creek *n.* 小河；小溪

6

The Constellations

From the beginning of time, people have been watching the sky. *Ancient* peoples saw that groups of stars appeared in different parts of the sky at different times of the year. Farmers used these groups to tell what season it was and when to plant. People used their imagination to name the groups. They

星座

自古以来，人们就观察天空，古人们看到在一年内的不同时间星星出现在天空的不同地方。农民利用这些不同的星群来辨别季节以及什么时候耕种，人们利用他们的想象来给星群命名，他们用动物、

---

ancient *adj.* 古代的

named them for animals, gods, objects, and characters from myths. These groups of stars are called *constellations*.

One well-known constellation is *Orion the Hunter*. It can be seen in North America on winter nights. In the southern part of the sky, there are three bright stars in a straight row. These make up Orion's belt. From the belt, other stars extend outward to form a *dagger*. At the shoulder is a bright star known as Betelgeuse. Orion's left foot is a star called Rigel.

A constellation that is easy to find is *Ursa Major*, or the Great Bear. The Great Bear can be seen year round in the northern sky. The Great Bear can be seen by first finding the Big Dipper. There are four stars that make up the bowl of the dipper. A line of stars makes up the handle. The bowl of the dipper forms a saddle on the back of the Great Bear. The handle of the dipper is the Great Bear's tail. Before

---

天神、物体和神话里的人物来命名。这些星群叫做星座。

一个比较著名的星座叫做猎户座。在北美洲冬天晚上能看到。天空的南方有三颗明亮的星星排成直线。这组成了猎户座的腰带。从腰带开始，其他星星向外延伸形成了一把剑。在肩部有一颗明亮的星星称为参宿四，在猎户座左脚的星星称为参宿七。

另一个比较容易被发现的星座是大熊星座或称大熊座。在天空的北部可以常年看到这个星座。我们首先找到北斗七星，这样我们就可以看到大熊星座。四颗星组成长柄勺的勺部分，一条线上的星星构成柄。在大熊星座的背面，长勺的勺形成了它的脊背，长柄勺的柄是大熊星座的尾部，在

---

constellation *n.* 星座
dagger *n.* 匕首；短剑

Orion the Hunter 猎户座
Ursa Major 大熊星座

the Civil War, a well-known song called *the Big Dipper the Drinking Gourd*. Slaves who tried to escape followed the Big Dipper to be sure they were going north.

The two stars at the pouring end of the Big Dipper are called *pointer* stars. This is because they point to the North Star. The North Star, also called Polaris, is in the same direction as the North Pole. Because of this, sailors and other people who traveled could always find the North Star and use it to tell them which way was north.

The North Star is part of a *constellation* called Ursa Minor, or the Little Bear. Part of the Little Bear is a group of stars called the *Little Dipper*. The bowl of the dipper is the Little Bear's side, and the handle is the Little Bear's tail. The North Star is at the very tip of the tail.

There are many more constellations named for animals. There are *Orion's dogs*, *Canis Major* and Canis Minor. They hunt Lepus the rabbit and Taurus the bull.

内战之前一首非常著名的歌叫《大熊星座的喝水葫芦》。设法逃脱的奴隶们跟着北斗七星，以确定他们是往北逃。

在北斗七星斗口部分的两颗星星叫做极星，因为它们指向北极星。北极星也叫做北晨，与北极同一个方向。利用这点，航行者和其他旅行的人总能找到北极星，并且告诉他们哪条路向北。

北极星是小熊星座的一部分，部分小熊星座组成了小北斗七星。北斗的勺部是小熊的侧面，把柄是小熊的尾巴。北极星在尾巴上的顶端。

还有很多以动物命名的星座，有猎户座的狗，大犬星座和小犬星座。它们猎捕天兔座和金牛座。

---

pointer *n.* 标志；指示
Little Dipper 小北斗七星

constellation *n.* 星座
Canis Major 大犬座

7

A Visit to a Planetarium

Yesterday, Ms. Kim's fourth-grade class visited a *planetarium*. It was a big round room with rows of seats in a circle and a *dome* overhead. While the class was getting seated, a student asked, "Where are the plants?"

Ms. Kim said, "The word planetarium comes from *planet*, not plant. We're here to

参观天文馆

昨天，金小姐的四年级参观了天文馆，天文馆就是一个有很多座位排在圆圈里的圆形房间，并有一个圆形屋顶。整个班级的同学都坐好了以后，一个同学就问："植物在哪儿？"

金小姐说："天文馆一词来源于星球，而不是植物。在这里我们可以认识了解星球和星星。在房间的中心有一个大球，大球是一个有很多洞

---

planetarium *n.* 天文馆；天象馆
planet *n.* 行星；星球

dome *n.* 圆屋顶；穹顶

learn about planets and stars." In the center of the room was a large *sphere*. It was a metal ball that was full of small holes. An *amiable* man walked in with a smile and started the program, which was called a sky show. He said that the dome was a big screen and the sphere was a star *projector*. A light in the projector shines through the holes and makes images of stars on the screen.

The room began to darken slowly, as if the Sun were going down. Finally it was very dark and the stars came out. "This is what the sky will look like at ten o'clock tonight," the man said. The students saw the planet Mars, which *glowed* red. They saw the stars of the Big Dipper and Orion. They learned that because Earth rotates, the stars appear to move across the sky during the night. Then they learned that because of the way Earth orbits the Sun, people see different stars at different times of the year. When the show was over, some students said they were going to look at the stars that night.

的金属球。一个亲切的人面带微笑走进来，开始了这个叫做"天空秀"的节目。他介绍说圆屋顶是一个非常大的屏幕，圆球是星星投影仪，投影仪中的一束束光通过洞在屏幕上形成星星的影像。

房间慢慢地变暗，好像太阳下山了，最后变得很暗，星星就出来了。"这就是晚上10点天空的样子"那个人说道。同学们看到了发红光的火星。同时看到了北斗星和猎户座。他们了解到地球旋转导致星星晚上的转动。由于地球围绕着太阳公转，人们会在一年不同的时间看到不同的星星。当这个节目结束时，一些同学说打算晚上观察星星。

---

sphere *n.* 球体
projector *n.* 放映机；投影仪

amiable *adj.* 和蔼可亲的
glow *v.* 发出暗淡的光；发红

8

Grow Your Own Vegetables

Vegetables from a garden are tastier and more nutritious than the ones sold at a store. Growing vegetables can be fun. You can ask an adult to help you plant them.

Step One: Find the following items: a sunny plot of ground, *fertilizer*, seeds, a *shovel*, a *rake*, a *hoe*, and water.

种属于自己的蔬菜

果园里面采摘的蔬菜要比在商店里面卖的味道更好，更有营养。种蔬菜很有意思。可以找一个成年人帮你种蔬菜。

第一步：找到以下东西。一块阳光充足的土地、肥料、种子、铲子、耙子、锄头和水。

---

fertilizer *n.* 肥料
rake *n.* 耙子

shovel *n.* 铲；铁铲
hoe *n.* 锄头

Step Two: Decide what to plant and when to plant it. Some vegetables that are easy to grow are tomatoes, *beets*, and *squash*. To find out when to plant, look in a garden book, or ask someone who knows a lot about gardens.

Step Three: Prepare the soil. Pull out grass and weeds. Then use a shovel to turn over the dirt and chop up any *lumps* in the soil. Rake up and remove roots and rocks.

Step Four: Use the hoe to mix fertilizer into the dirt.

Step Five: Plant your seeds in rows. Make a small hole in the ground with your finger. Drop the seed in the hole and cover it with soil. Read the seed packages to see how deep to plant each kind of seed.

第二步：决定你想要种什么，什么时候种。有一些植物很容易生长，像西红柿、甜菜和南瓜。在种植书上查看什么时候开始种，或是向懂得很多种植知识的人员询问。

第三步：准备好土。拔出杂草。用铲子翻地，打碎结块的土。用耙子移走藤蔓和石块。

第四步：用锄头将肥料混合在泥土中。

第五步：种子播种成行。用手指在地面上挖一个小洞。把种子撒在洞里面，然后再盖上土。阅读种子包装上的说明，看看深度多少适合种这种蔬菜。

---

beet *n.* 甜菜　　　　　　　　　　　　　　　　squash *n.* 南瓜小果

lump *n.* 块

Step Six: Water your vegetable garden every day.

Step Seven: As your vegetables start to grow, watch for weeds and pull them out.

Step Eight: Pick your vegetables when they are *ripe* and ready to eat.

Step Nine: Enjoy!

第六步：每天给菜园浇水。

第七步：植物开始生长，观察有没有野草，然后把它们拔出。

第八步：成熟的时候采摘下来准备享用。

第九步：尽情享用吧！

---

ripe *adj.* 成熟的

9

What Is a Veterinarian?

A *veterinarian* is an animal doctor. Veterinarians are also called vets. They treat animals that are sick or hurt and they help healthy animals stay well.

Some vets treat small animals, such as cats, dogs, birds, and *hamsters*. Many vets who treat small animals work at pet clinics. People bring their pets in to see the

什么是兽医?

兽医就是动物医生，兽医也叫"vets,"他们治疗受伤或是生病的动物，并且帮助动物保持健康。

有些兽医治疗小动物，例如：猫、狗、小鸟儿以及仓鼠。许多兽医在宠物医院治疗小动物。人们带着宠物去看兽医。兽医给看似健康的动物做全面的身体检查。假设患者是一只狗，兽医检查狗的皮毛，检查是否有跳蚤以及皮肤问题。同样也检查狗的耳朵和牙齿。兽医通过检查皮肤感觉体

---

veterinarian *n.* 兽医   hamster *n.* 仓鼠

vet. Vets give checkups to patients that seem healthy. Suppose the patient is a dog. The vet looks at the dog's hair and skin. This is to check for fleas or skin problems. The vet looks into the dog's ears and checks its teeth. The vet checks the inside of the dog by feeling its organs through the skin.

Vets also teach pet owners how to take care of their pets. Vets keep pets from getting sick by giving them *shots* or other protective medicine. They clean their patients' teeth and perform surgery. One kind of surgery is to *spay* or *neuter* dogs and cats so they can't have unwanted puppies or kittens. Vets also operate to take out *tumors*. They fix broken bones and mend other injuries.

Some vets treat farm animals. These include horses, cows, sheep, pigs, goats, and chickens. These vets go to farms to see their patients. They must carry all of their supplies with them. They may

内器官是否生病。

兽医同时也指导宠物的主人怎样照顾宠物。通过给动物打针或是吃药能够防止动物生病。清理动物的牙齿或给动物患者进行手术。有一种手术就是将猫狗阉割，这样就不会生小狗小猫了。同样兽医也可以做摘除肿瘤、接骨以及其他伤口的治疗手术。

一些兽医治疗农场的动物，这些动物包括马、奶牛、羊、猪、山羊和鸡等。这些医生上门出诊。出诊时必须带上他们所用的设备。他们可能需要对奶牛群做一些疾病的测试。在奶牛群中给每头奶牛都打上一针。也可

shot *n.* 注射
neuter *v.* 阉割

spay *v.* 切除（雌畜）卵巢
tumor *n.* 肿瘤

need to test a *herd* of cows for disease. They may give a shot to every cow in the herd. They may help a horse give birth to a *foal* or *stitch* a cut on a pig's leg. They may even perform surgery in a barn.

Other vets take care of zoo animals. A zoo vet has to treat many kinds of animals. These can include fish, bears, snakes, and *seals*. Zoo vets might give a zebra a checkup or operate on an elephant. They might clean a lion's teeth or trim a bird's toenails. Before working on large zoo animals, vets first put them to sleep. They do this by shooting darts into their bodies. The darts contain drugs. When the vet is finished working on an animal, he or she gives the animal a shot to wake it up.

It takes years of schooling to be a vet. First, students must take college courses. Then they must go to a school of veterinary medicine and earn a Doctor of Veterinary Medicine degree. All vets have one thing in common. They care about animals.

能给马接生，或者给猪缝合受伤的腿，他们甚至在仓库中就可以出色地完成手术。

另一些兽医在动物园里照顾动物。动物园里的兽医需要照顾各种动物。这些动物包括：鱼、熊、蛇以及海豹。动物园兽医可能给斑马做全身检查，给大象做手术，给狮子清理牙齿，给鸟剪指甲。兽医给大动物做手术之前，首先让它们昏睡，这是通过用飞镖枪向动物发镖注射药物完成的，当工作完成时，兽医会给动物打针让它们醒来。

成为兽医之前要学习很多年。首先，学生需要学习很多大学的课程，然后他们学习兽医学，获得兽医博士学位。所有的兽医都有一个共同点，就是爱护小动物。

---

herd *n.* 兽群；牧群   foal *n.* 小马驹

stitch *v.* 缝合；缝补   seal *n.* 海豹

10

Are Dogs Getting Healthier?

Dogs are living longer. Twenty years ago, people considered a 12-year-old dog to be very old. Today, many dogs live to be 15 or older. Dogs live 25 percent longer now than they did then! There are two *main* causes for this change. Dogs eat better food, and they get better health care.

In the 1970s, more people began treating dogs as members of their families. People

狗更健康了吗?

狗的寿命越来越长了。20年前，人们认为12岁的狗非常老了，而今天，很多狗都能活到15岁或更长寿命。狗比20年前多活25%的寿命。主要有两个原因导致这些事情的改变。它们吃得越来越好，得到更好的治疗保健。

在20世纪70年代，越来越多的人把狗当成家庭成员。为了照顾好小狗，他们花更多的钱。其他事情也慢慢发生改变。狗粮公司卖的狗粮种类

---

main *adj.* 主要的

spent more money to keep their dogs well. Then, other things began to change. Dog-food companies sold more kinds of food for dogs. Puppies, adult dogs, and old dogs need different kinds of food. Some dog foods contain medicines that help prevent diseases.

At the same time, more people began taking their dogs to the vet for checkups. If a problem is found early, it can be treated before it does much damage to the dog. Many dogs used to die from heart disease that was caused by *germs* from diseased *gums*. People began to have their dogs' teeth cleaned. More people had their dogs spayed and neutered. Spayed or neutered dogs cannot have unwanted pups. They also are less *susceptible* to some kinds of cancer. More people stopped letting their dogs run *loose*. Fewer dogs were hit by cars. New and better medicines were developed. They kept dogs from dying of diseases that used to kill many dogs. Now dog owners can have their best friends with them longer.

越来越多。小狗，成年狗和老狗需要不同的食物，一些狗粮中含有防治疾病的药物。

同时，越来越多的人带着狗去做身体检查，使问题尽早发现，在对狗造成更多伤害之前治好。很多狗死于心脏类疾病。这些都是由患病的牙龈上的细菌引起的。人们开始给狗清理牙齿。更多的人给狗进行阉割手术。手术过的狗不能再生育小狗，同时也可以减少癌症的发生。更多的人不让他们的狗乱跑，减少狗被车撞死的机率。人们生产出更新效果更好的药物，这些都防止狗死于那些致命的疾病。现在狗的主人能与人类最好的朋友待更长的时间。

---

germ *n.* 细菌；病菌

susceptible *adj.* 易受影响的（或受伤等）

gum *n.* 牙龈；牙床

loose *adj.* 不受约束的；未束缚的

11

The Features of Earth's Surface

The surface of Earth is *wrinkled* with mountains and *carved* out with valleys. In some places the surface is flat. Earth is crossed by rivers and dotted with lakes. Much of it is covered by ocean.

All of Earth's land and ocean sit on a layer of rock. This layer is called the *lithosphere*. The lithosphere is made up of

地球表面的特征

地球表面是皱起的高山和凹陷的山谷。有一些地方是平坦的。地球上有纵横交错的河流和斑斑点点的湖泊。地球表面大部分被海洋所覆盖。

地球所有的陆地和海洋都在一个岩层上面。这个岩层就叫做岩石圈。这个岩石圈是由许多不同的板块构成的。板块之间巨大的裂痕就是断层。

---

wrinkle v. （使）起皱褶   carve v. 雕刻
lithosphere n. 岩石圈

sections called plates. Large cracks between plates are called *faults*. Plates move because of pressure from deep within Earth. When plates press against each other, they can push up layers of rock, which is how some mountains are created. When plates move apart, they can cause large blocks of Earth's surface to sink.

Other mountains are made by volcanoes. Melted rock called *magma* moves up from deep inside Earth. As it rises, it gives off gases. These gases push on Earth's surface and cause it to *bulge*. When the pressure gets very high, the gas explodes out of the ground. The magma that comes out of the volcano is called *lava*. The volcano erupts again and again, and the lava builds up to form a mountain. Sometimes many years pass between eruptions.

地球深处的压力引起地球板块的移动。当板块间相互碰撞，就会将岩层向上推，这时山就出现了。当板块相互移开了，就会引起地球表面的大块下沉。

也有一些高山是由火山喷发形成的。熔化了的岩石叫做岩浆，岩浆会从地球表面喷发出来。岩浆上升，释放出气体，气体推向地表，在表面形成隆起。当压力足够大时，气体从地表喷发，从火山中流出来的岩浆叫做熔岩。火山一次又一次地爆发，岩浆冷凝后形成了高山。有时火山喷发中间要隔许多年。

---

fault *n.* （地壳岩层的）断层　　　　magma *n.* 岩浆；熔岩

bulge *v.* 凸出，鼓胀　　　　　　　lava *n.* （火山喷出的）熔岩；岩浆

Land can also be shaped by *erosion*. Erosion occurs when water or wind wears away softer rock and leaves behind harder rock. After a long, long time, the harder rock may stand alone as mountains. Sometimes it appears as the walls of *canyons*.

Water moves from high ground to low ground. Small streams can come together to form large streams. Large streams can join to form rivers. Rivers flow into lakes or the ocean.

The ocean is a huge body of salt water that covers almost three-fourths of Earth. The ocean is divided into smaller oceans and seas. On the ocean floor are the midocean *ridges*. These are chains of mountains formed by volcanoes. There are many large *cracks* between the ridges. As some of the cracks widen, magma comes up and forms new mountains. Many islands are volcanoes that have

---

地球表面也可能通过侵蚀形成。有风或水时会发生侵蚀，它们会侵蚀较软的岩层，之后会留下坚硬的岩层。很长一段时间过去后，较坚硬的岩层会独自留下，形成高山。有时这些岩层也会形成峡谷。

水从高处流向低处，小溪汇聚成大溪流，大的溪流涌成河流，河流流向湖泊或是海洋。

海洋是一个巨大的咸水集合体。大约覆盖地表的四分之三。海洋分成一些小海洋和海。在海底有海脊。这些海脊山链是火山喷发形成的。在海脊之间有很多断层。由于其中的一些断层不断扩大，岩浆就会喷出，形成一些新的山。许多小岛都是由海中的火山高出海面形成的。夏威夷就是这

---

erosion *n.* 腐蚀；侵蚀

ridge *n.* 脊；垄

canyon *n.* 峡谷

crack *n.* 裂缝；缝隙

risen above the surface of the ocean. Hawaii was formed this way.

The surface of Earth is always changing. At one time, all land was in one place. The ocean covered the rest of the world. As the plates slowly moved, the land broke apart. Ocean water moved between the *masses* of land. Over a long period of time, the *continents* we know today were formed.

样的岛。

地表总是在不停变化的。从前所有的陆地板块都是在一个地方。其他地方被海洋所覆盖。当板块开始移动，陆地就开始分裂。海洋里的水在陆地板块之间流动。经历很长的时期，今天我们所知道的各大洲就形成了。

---

mass *n.* 块；大量   continent *n.* 大陆；洲

12

Down the Mississippi River

Last summer, my family took a river trip down the Mississippi. The river starts out as a small creek that flows from a lake in Minnesota. We began our trip at St. Paul, the capital of Minnesota. There the river is wide enough for bigger boats. After we left St. Paul, we saw some *cormorants*. These are birds that eat fish and swim. While Mom watched them dive for fish, Dad saw an eagle.

沿密西西比顺流而下

去年夏天，我们家人进行了一次沿着密西西比顺流而下的旅行。这条河的起源是明尼苏达州的一个湖泊流出的一个小溪流。我们在明尼苏达州的首府圣保罗开始了旅程。这条河对我们的船来说足够宽。当我们离开圣保罗，看到了一些鸬鹚。这些鸟儿吃鱼，并会游泳。当妈妈看它们潜水捕鱼时，爸爸看到了一只鹰。

cormorant *n.* 鸬鹚

Farther south, we saw a sign on the riverbank where Minnesota, Iowa, and Wisconsin meet. As we went on, we saw islands and *sandbars*. The river has lots of twists and turns. It widened as we went farther south. This is because more rivers *merge* with it. Also, it collects water that runs off the land. One day, we saw a *tugboat* pushing 15 *barges*. Barges are flat ships that carry goods. Later on we saw tugs with 50 barges. Once, when we were south of Baton Rouge, Louisiana, we saw ocean ships on the river. As we got close to New Orleans, I saw two alligators.

Our trip ended in New Orleans, but the Mississippi River runs on to the Gulf of Mexico. The river is more than 3,200 kilometers (2,000 miles) long. It flows along the borders of 10 states!

再往南，我们看到了河岸上的一个路标，是明尼苏达州、爱荷华州和威斯康星州交汇处。我们继续向前走，看到了岛和沙洲。这条河曲曲折折的。在南边它变宽了，这是因为更多的河流汇聚。它也汇集很多陆地上流下的水流。有一天我们看到了一条拖船推着15条驳船。驳船就是一些平底的可以运载货物的船。随后我们又看到推着50条驳船的拖船。有一次，我们在路易斯安那州的巴吞鲁日南面看到了一条远洋船。当我们接近新奥尔良时，我们又看到了两条鳄鱼。

我们的旅行在新奥尔良结束了，然而密西西比河最后涌入墨西哥湾。这条河有3 200多千米（2 000英尺）长，流过10个州。

---

sandbar *n.* （河口的）沙洲
tugboat *n.* 拖船

merge *v.* 合并；并入
barge *n.* 驳船

13

Simple Machines

A machine is a *device* that helps
people to do more work than
they can do by themselves. When you
think of a machine, you probably think of
something that has many parts. But some
machines have only one or two parts.
These are called simple machines. Simple
machines make it easier to move heavy

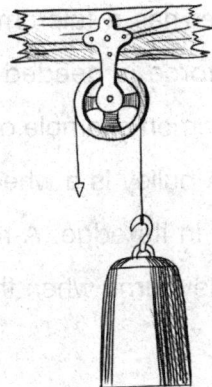

简单机械

机械就是一种可以帮助我们做更多工作的装置。当你想到一个机械的时候，可能想到它有很多的零部件。但是有些机械只有一个或是两个零部件，这些机械称为简单机械。简单机械可以使搬运变得很

---

device *n.* 装置；仪器

objects. Some of the most common simple machines are *levers*, pulleys, and *inclined* planes.

A lever is a rod. When using a lever, a person transfers a force from one end of the rod to the other. This is done by putting the rod on a *fulcrum*, which is a point that stays still. One kind of lever is a seesaw. Here the fulcrum is in the middle. A seat is at each end of the rod. When you push down on one end, you raise the weight on the other end. If the lever has a fulcrum that is close to one end, only a small amount of force is needed at the other end to move the object. Another common example of a lever is a *crowbar*.

A pulley is a wheel that turns on an axle. The wheel has a groove cut in its edge. A rope runs through the groove. The wheel of the pulley turns when the rope is pulled. Pulleys are usually attached to

---

容易。一些最普通的简单机械有杠杆、滑轮和斜面。

杠杆就是一根棒。当我们使用杠杆时，我们可以使力从一端转移到另一端。这是通过把杠杆安在一个支点上，支点不动，就实现了力的转移。跷跷板就是一个杠杆的应用。在杆的中间安有一个支点，在杆的两端安有座椅。当你在一端压低，就会增加另一端的重量，如果支点接近另一端，用一个很小的力就足可以抬起另一端的物品。另一个关于杠杆的应用实例就是撬棍。

滑轮就是可以绕着一个轴运动的轮子，在轮子的侧边有一个槽，绳子可以在槽里缠绕转动。当拉动绳子的时候，轮子就转动起来。滑轮通常都

---

lever *n.* 杠杆
fulcrum *n.* （杠杆的）支点；支轴

incline *v.* 使倾向于
crowbar *n.* 撬棍

high places, such as a wooden *beam* on the ceiling of a *warehouse*. A person ties one end of the rope around a heavy object and pulls on the other end. The wheel changes the direction of the force that is created when the person pulls on the rope. The pulley makes it easier to lift the object, because it is easier to pull down on a rope with a heavy load than to pull the load up.

An inclined plane is a straight, *slanted* surface, such as a *ramp*. It is easier to push an object up a ramp than it is to lift an object straight up in the air. The longer the ramp, the easier it is to move the object. This is because the pull of gravity is stronger against something moving straight up than it is against something moving diagonally on a ramp. Another example of an inclined plane is a road that runs uphill. The steeper the road, the more difficult it is to walk up.

安装在较高的地方，例如，仓库天花板的木梁上。人们把绳子的一段绑着重物，拉动另一端。当人拉动绳子的时候改变了力的方向。通过滑轮可以很容易地拉起重物。因为向下拉动绳子要比向上拉起东西容易得多。

斜面通常就是一个直的倾斜的板面，像是斜坡。通过斜面推动物品要比在空中抬起物品容易得多。斜面越长，越容易搬运物品。这是因为重力阻止物体在垂直方向上运动的作用比阻止物体在斜面上的运动更强烈。斜面的另一个应用实例就是上坡的路面，越是陡峭越是很难向上攀爬。

---

beam *n.* 梁
slant *v.* 倾斜

warehouse *n.* 仓库；货仓
ramp *n.* 斜坡；坡道

14

A Simple Solution

Tony and Jennifer sat on the floor of their tree house playing cards. Jennifer said, "I wish we had some chairs."

"We could get those two big *beanbag* chairs in the basement," Tony suggested.

Jennifer looked out the window and down at the ground. She said, "We can't carry them while we climb up here." They decided to pull the chairs up with a rope.

一个简单的解决方法

托尼和詹妮弗坐在他们树屋的地板上打牌。詹妮弗说："我们要是有一些椅子就好了。"

托尼建议说"我们可以从地下室搬两个豆袋椅。"

詹妮弗从窗外看向地面说："我们爬上来的时候搬不了豆袋椅。"他们决定用一根绳子把椅子拉上来。

---

beanbag *n.* 豆袋坐垫；豆子袋

Jennifer went to find a long rope while Tony got the chairs. They tied the rope around one of the chairs. They took the other end of the rope and climbed up to the tree house. They *tugged* on the rope, but it was very hard to *hoist* the chair. When the chair was only halfway up, their arms got tired, and they had to let go of the rope. Then Jennifer remembered seeing a *pulley* on their dad's *workbench*. Their dad brought a ladder and attached the pulley to the tree house, just above the window. Jennifer threaded the rope around the pulley.

On the ground, Tony tied one end of the rope to a chair. He pulled on the other end of the rope. It was easy to lift the chair. When it got up to the tree house, Jennifer pulled it inside. Then Tony tied the rope around the other chair and moved it up to the tree house too. "My arms aren't even tired!" he yelled happily.

詹妮弗找到了一根长绳，托尼搬来椅子。他们用绳子绑着一把椅子，握住绳子的另一端，然后他们爬上树。他们用力拉绳子，但是很难把椅子拉起来。当椅子拉到一半时，他们的胳膊就没力气了，他们只能松开绳子。这时詹妮弗想起了爸爸的工作台上有一个滑轮。爸爸拿来了一把梯子，然后把滑轮安装在树屋的窗子上面。詹妮弗把绳子绕过滑轮。

在地面上，托尼用绳子的一端绑上椅子。他拉动绳子的另一端。很容易就举起了椅子。当椅子升到树屋时，詹妮弗把椅子拉到里面。然后托尼用绳子绑另一把椅子，用同样的方法搬运到树屋内。他开心地叫喊着，"我的胳膊一点儿也不累。"

---

tug *v.* 拉；拽
pulley *n.* 滑轮；滑轮组

hoist *v.* 吊起；拉高
workbench *n.* 工作台

15

The Scientific Discoveries of Benjamin Franklin

Scientists ask questions. They want to know why something happens. To find out, they watch what happens and then think of an idea that explains how and why it works. This idea is called a *hypothesis*. Once a scientist has a hypothesis, he or she performs an experiment to see if the hypothesis is correct.

本杰明·富兰克林的科学发现

科学家提出问题。他们想要弄清楚事情为什么会发生。为了找出结果，他们会观察发生了什么，然后思考它是怎样工作的，为什么这样运行。这种想法就是假说。一旦科学家提出了一个假说，他或她要完成一个实验去验证假说是否正确。

---

hypothesis *n.* 假说；假设

Benjamin Franklin was a scientist. He lived in the 1700s. At that time, people did not understand what lightning was. Franklin thought that it was the same thing as electricity. It was known that electricity could make *sparks*. If Franklin could get lightning to make sparks, then he would prove that lightning and electricity were the same thing.

Franklin thought that he could use a kite to attract lightning from a cloud. He built his kite out of two wooden sticks and a large silk handkerchief. He put a piece of pointed metal at the top of the kite. He tied a key to the end of the kite string. When a storm was coming, he went out in a field where there was a small *shed*. He got the kite up and then stood in the shed. When he saw that the threads of the string were beginning to *stand on end*, he touched the

本杰明·富兰克林是一名科学家，他生活在18世纪。那时，人们不知道闪电是什么。富兰克林认为闪电和电是一样的。众所周知电可以产生电火花。如果富兰克林可以用闪电制造出电火花来，那么他就可以证明闪电和电是相同的东西。

富兰克林想用一个风筝从云层中吸引闪电。他用两根木棍和一个丝绸的围巾制成了一个风筝。他把一个尖的金属块放在了风筝的顶上，在风筝绳的末尾安放了一把钥匙。当暴风雨来临时，他就走到一个搭有小棚的地方。他站在小棚里放起风筝。当他看到风筝线开始竖立起来时，他就用手指去触碰

spark n. 火花 　　　　　　　　　　shed n. 简易房；棚
stand on end　竖立；直立

key with his *knuckle*. He saw a spark. Before the rain had ended, he was able to get many more sparks.

Franklin made other important scientific discoveries. Years before he flew his kite, he had thought it possible to predict which way storms would move. To learn more about storms, he chased a *whirlwind* on horseback. On the basis of what he found out, Franklin made weather forecasts. He was also a printer, so he published his forecasts.

In his lifetime, Franklin sailed across the Atlantic Ocean to Europe eight times. Onboard ship, he was curious about ocean *currents*. On each trip, he took the temperature of the water. He used his findings

---

钥匙。他看到了火花。在雨结束前，他看到了更多的电火花。

富兰克林也有其他很重要的科学发现。在做风筝实验的前些年，他就在思考预测暴风雨的移动路径。为了学习更多关于暴风雨的知识，他在马背上追逐旋风。在这些发现的基础上他还对天气进行了预测。他还是一个印刷工，出版了这些预报。

在他的一生中，他八次穿越大西洋到欧洲去。在船上，他对洋流产生了兴趣。每次旅行，他都带着水温计。他根据他的发现绘制出海洋最重要

---

knuckle *n.* 指节；指关节   whirlwind *n.* 旋风；旋流

current *n.* 水流；潮流

to *chart* one of the ocean's most important currents, the Gulf Stream.

Like some other great scientists, Franklin was an inventor too. He used what he learned· from science to invent things to make people's lives safer and easier. He invented the lightning rod. A lightning rod can keep buildings and ships from being damaged by lightning. He built a wood *stove* to heat homes. It used less wood and was safer than a *fireplace*.

的一支洋流——墨西哥湾暖流。

同其他的科学家一样，富兰克林也是个发明家。他用所学习的知识发明了一些能使人们生活更安全更便捷的东西。他发明了避雷针。避雷针可以使建筑和船只免受雷电的袭击。他发明了柴火炉取暖。柴火炉使用较少的木材，比壁炉更安全。

---

chart *v.* 绘制区域地图　　　　　　　　stove *n.* （用于取暖的）炉子；火炉
fireplace *n.* 壁炉

16

How Do Kites Fly?

When you watch a colorful kite fly against a blue sky, do you wonder how it stays up there? It takes wind to fly a kite. Wind has force. The surface of a kite is *curved*. As the wind blows across a curved surface, it causes an increase in air pressure. The surface of the kite is facing downward, and so the pressure *underneath*

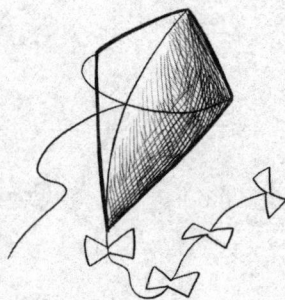

风筝是怎样飞行的呢?

你看到五颜六色的风筝在蓝天上飞翔时，你会想它是怎样悬在那的吗? 借助风来放风筝。风提供了推动力。风筝的表面是弯曲的。风吹过风筝的弯曲的表面，引起空气压力的增大。风筝的表面朝

---

curved *adj.* 呈弯曲状的；弧形的   underneath *prep.* 在……底下

the kite is high. The pressure pushes the kite upward.

A kite cannot rise forever because of the string to which it is attached. As a person lets out more and more string, the weight of the string increases. If the weight of the string in the air gets close to the weight of the kite, the kite will start to *descend*.

Kites weigh very little, so it doesn't take much wind to lift them. Sometimes a kite is so light that it needs a tail to add weight and balance to keep it from *tumbling* and turning.

Kites come in lots of shapes, but they all have curved surfaces. A flat kite wouldn't fly because there would be no lift.

People have been flying kites for about 2,500 years. Kites were the first type of aircraft.

下，在下面的压力大。压力推着风筝升高。

由于风筝拴着绳子，所以风筝不能无限制地升高。尽管我们可以放更长的绳子，但是绳子的重量也会增加。如果绳子的重量接近风筝，那么风筝就会下降。

风筝的重量很小，所以风不大的时候就能放风筝。有时候风筝太轻了，所以要添加一个尾巴增加风筝的重量来保持风筝平衡而不翻滚。

风筝有许多的形状，但是它们都有弯曲的表面。平面的风筝不能飞，因为没有上升力。

人类在大约2 500年以前就发明了风筝。风筝是第一种航空器。

---

descend *v.* 下降；下去　　　　　　tumble *v.* 滚落；翻滚下来

17

The Truth About Sharks

There are many *myths*, or false ideas, about sharks. One is that sharks like to eat people. Although some sharks can eat people, we really aren't on their menu. Sharks usually eat fish or sea *mammals* such as seals, especially if the fish or mammals are weak or dead.

The whale shark is Earth's biggest fish.

有关鲨鱼的真相

关于鲨鱼有很多错误的看法，或者说错误的观念。其中的一个就是鲨鱼喜欢吃人。尽管鲨鱼能够吃人，但是我们真的不在它们的菜单上。鲨鱼经常吃一些鱼类或是像海豹这样的哺乳动物，特别是虚弱的或是已死亡的鱼类或是哺乳动物。

鲸鲨是地球上最大的鱼。尽管鲸比较大，但它们是哺乳动物，而不是

---

myth *n.* 虚构的东西；荒诞的说法   mammal *n.* 哺乳动物

Although whales are bigger, they are mammals, not fish. The great white shark is perhaps the most dangerous to people. Great whites are large sharks and are known to attack people. These attacks are rare. It is believed that they happen when a shark mistakes a person for something else.

Because sharks have been around since ancient times, they are thought to be *primitive*, simple animals. This is another myth. Sharks are really very *complicated*. They have a powerful sense of smell and sharp hearing. Some have organs on their snouts that pick up electric currents made by themuscles of swimming fish. Sharks have large brains, and they learn quickly. They have a memory and can be trained. Many sharks have rows of sharp teeth. When teeth are lost, other teeth move in to replace them.

鱼类。对人类来说大白鲨可能是最危险的。大白鲨是大的鲨鱼，以攻击人类而被人所熟悉。这样的攻击是罕见的。据说鲨鱼把人当成了其他的东西才会发生攻击现象。

由于鲨鱼从远古时代就出现了，所以它们被认为是最原始的、简单的动物。这就是关于鲨鱼的另一个误解。实际上鲨鱼是非常复杂的。鲨鱼有发达的嗅觉和敏锐的听觉。有些鲨鱼的鼻子上有一些器官能够收集到鱼游动时由肌肉所产生的电流。鲨鱼有很大的大脑，所以鲨鱼学得很快。它们有记忆，而且可以被训练。很多鲨鱼都有成排的锋利的牙齿。当某些牙齿脱落老化，就会长出新的牙齿代替它们。

---

primitive *adj.* 原始的；远古的   complicated *adj.* 复杂的；难懂的

Another myth about sharks is that they don't see very well. Actually, sharks have good vision, especially in dim light. They have a layer of *cells* at the back of the eye that works like a mirror to *strengthen* the light.

One myth that was created by movies is that when a shark is getting ready to attack, you can see its back *fin* above the water. The truth is that a shark often attacks from below, without showing its fin above the surface.

Sharks have a reputation as being dangerous, and so some people think it would be better if there were no sharks at all. This is a bad idea. Sharks are *scavengers*. They clean up garbage from ships and waste from the ocean. They help other species of sea animals stay strong by eating animals that are sick or weak.

另一个关于鲨鱼的误解就是它们的视力不好。事实上，鲨鱼有很好的视力，特别是在昏暗的条件下。鲨鱼的眼睛后部有类似镜子的能够加强光线的一层细胞。

有一个错误的观念是通过电影形成的，那就是当鲨鱼准备攻击人类的时候，可以看见它的背鳍露出水面。但事实是，鲨鱼发起攻击的时候在较低处，并且它的背鳍不会露出水面。

鲨鱼被认为是危险的，所以有些人认为若没有鲨鱼会更好。这是一个错误的想法。鲨鱼是食腐动物。它们清除船只产生的垃圾和海洋废物。通过捕食老弱动物使其他物种保持强壮。

---

cell *n.* 细胞
fin *n.* （鱼的）鳍

strengthen *v.* 加强；增强
scavenger *n.* 食腐肉的兽（或鸟）

Much of what we know about sharks comes from the scientists who have studied them. Dr. Eugenie Clark has made many dives to study sharks. She has also studied sharks in her lab. For example, she trained them to press a *target* to get food and learned how sharks can *identify* color and shape. Because of her work with sharks, Clark is known as the Shark Lady.

我们所知道的关于鲨鱼的了解大多数来自科学家对鲨鱼的研究。欧仁妮·克拉克博士多次潜水去研究鲨鱼。她也在实验室里面进行鲨鱼研究。例如：她训练鲨鱼通过按压靶来获取食物进而研究鲨鱼对颜色和形状的识别。由于她对鲨鱼的研究，克拉克被称为"鲨鱼夫人"。

target *n.* 目标；靶子　　　　　　　identify *v.* 确认；认出

18

The Crittercam

One day Greg Marshall was exploring a coral reef when a shark swam by. It had a *remora* stuck to it. A remora is a fish that attaches itself to the skin of bigger fish to get a free ride. Marshall wished that he could observe the shark's life as well as the remora could. He had an idea. Why couldn't a camera be attached to a shark,

动物摄影机

一天，格雷格·马歇尔在探索珊瑚礁时一条鲨鱼游过。有一个障碍挡住了鲨鱼。这个障碍就是一条使自己吸附在更大的鱼的皮肤上来获得免费旅行的鱼。马歇尔希望自己能像这个障碍物一样来观察鲨鱼的生活。于是他有了一个想法。为什么不能有个像障碍物这样的相机吸

remora *n.* 障碍

just like a remora? This is how the *Crittercam* was born.

The Crittercam is shaped like a *torpedo*, so it *slides* smoothly through the water. It does not bother the shark. It is secured to the shark in a way that does not hurt its skin. The Crittercam takes videos and sends signals. These signals allow scientists in a boat to track the shark's movements. The Crittercam can record how deep and how fast the shark swims. After a while, the wire attached to the Crittercam *dissolves* in the salt water. Then the boat picks up the Crittercam.

Marshall used the Crittercam on white sharks for a film. The videos showed how sharks hunt. From far below the surface, sharks watch for shadows above them. Then they strike.

附在鲨鱼身上呢？这样，第一台动物摄影机就产生了。

这台动物摄影机的形状就像是个鱼雷，这样就能在水中滑动自如。它没有使鲨鱼感到烦恼。从某种方面来说它能保护鲨鱼的皮肤不受伤害。动物摄影机带有摄影功能，能够发送信号。这些信号能够发送给船上的科学家来监测鲨鱼的行动。这个动物摄影机能够记录鲨鱼游的深度和游行速度。一段时间之后，系在动物摄影机上的绳索就会溶解在海水中，然后乘船就可以拿回动物摄影机。

马歇尔把动物摄影机吸附在白鲨上拍了一部电影。从影片中可以看到鲨鱼是怎样捕食的。从远处鲨鱼在水下就观察它们上面的影子，然后发动攻击。

---

crittercam *n.* 动物摄像机
slide *v.* （使）滑行；滑动

torpedo *n.* 鱼雷
dissolve *v.* 溶解

Before the Crittercam, a shark could be tracked only *briefly*. Now scientists can watch a shark's every move and see what it sees. The Crittercam can be used on other animals, both in the sea and on land.

在动物摄影机出现之前，人们只能进行短时间跟踪鲨鱼。现在科学家可以观察鲨鱼的每个动作，还可以看到鲨鱼看到的东西。动物摄影机还可以应用在其他海洋或是陆地上的动物身上。

briefly *adv.* 短暂地；暂时地

19

Types of Clouds

Have you ever watched clouds on a summer day? One cloud might look like a *woolly* sheep, while another one might remind you of a dog's tail. Some clouds might look like ocean waves or mountains. When you look at clouds, you will notice that there are many different kinds. Some clouds are high and thin, some are white and *fluffy*, and others look dark and heavy.

云的种类

你观察过夏天的云朵吗？一朵云有时候看起来像是一头绵羊，有时另一朵又让你想起了狗的尾巴。有些云朵像是海洋里的浪花或是山峰。当你观察云朵时，你可以注意到有很多不同种类的云。有些又高又薄，有些颜色又白又毛茸茸的，有些则看起来又黑又重。

woolly *adj.* 有毛覆盖的   fluffy *adj.* 绒毛般的

There are four kinds of clouds. They are high clouds, middle clouds, low clouds, and clouds that grow *vertically*. The clouds in these groups are named for the way they look.

Cirrus clouds are high clouds that are more than 5 kilometers (3 miles) above Earth. The air that high in the sky is very cold. Cirrus clouds are made of ice *crystals* that are so light that the wind blows them into thin strands. The word cirrus means "curl of hair." Some high clouds that look like layers or sheets are called cirrostratus clouds. The word stratus means "layer." There are other high clouds that look like clumps of cotton. These are the cirrocumulus clouds. Cumulus means "heap".

About 3 to 6.5 kilometers (2 to 4 miles) above Earth are the middle

---

有四种云，分别是高云、中云、低云和直展云。这些是依据云的样子来命名的。

卷云是高云的一种，距地球5千多米（3英里），在高空中空气很冷。卷云是由很轻的小冰晶组成，所以风可以把它们吹得很薄，一缕一缕的。卷云这个单词的意思是"卷曲的头发"。有一些高云看起来像是阶梯或是大片状的，它们是卷层云。层云的意思是"阶梯"。也有一些其他的高云看起来像是一团团的棉花。这些云朵是卷积云的一种。积云的意思是"堆积"。

在距离地球3到6.5千米（2到4英里）的云朵是中云。高层云是浅灰

---

vertically *adv.* 垂直地；直立地   cirrus *n.* 卷云
crystal *n.* 结晶；晶体

clouds. *Altostratus* clouds are light gray and can form a layer that looks like a blanket. *Altocumulus* clouds are very fluffy. They often are scattered across the sky. Another cloud that sometimes can be a middle cloud is the *nimbostratus* cloud. Nimbo comes from the word nimbus, which means "heavy rain." These clouds make a gray layer from which rain and snow falls. Nimbostratus clouds also can be low clouds.

The low clouds are no higher than about 1.6 kilometers (1 mile) above Earth. Two kinds of clouds are often found here. *Stratocumulus* clouds are light and dark and are made up of piles of fluffy clouds. Stratus clouds are very low clouds that spread out in a gray layer. They often give off moisture in the form of drizzle. Sometimes clouds form very close to the ground and become fog.

色的，可以形成一个毛毯状的阶梯。高积云非常蓬松，它们通常分散在天空中。另一种可能是中云的云朵是雨层云一词。"Nimbo"来源于雨云一词，意味着"暴雨"。这些云朵在下雨或下雪时形成灰黑色云层。雨层云也可以是低云。

　　低云距离地球表面不会超过1.6千米（1英尺）。低云通常有两种。层积云是灰白色的，由大量的蓬松的云朵组成。层云是在低空铺张开的灰色云层。它们以下毛毛雨的形式放出水分。有时候云层非常接近地面，在低空形成雾。

---

altostratus *n.* 高层云　　　　　altocumulus *n.* 高积云
nimbostratus *n.* 雨层云　　　　stratocumulus *n.* 层积云

The fourth group of clouds grows vertically. These clouds have a base near the ground but rise to a great height. Cumulus clouds can pile up on top of one another. When they pile up high, they are called *cumulonimbus* clouds. These cloud towers can rise as high as 18 kilometers (11 miles)! Cumulonimbus clouds are also known as *thunderheads* because they bring thunderstorms.

第四种云纵向生长。这些云朵的底部离地面非常近，但是会长得很高。积云可以一个堆积在另一个上面，当它们堆积得很高的时候就叫做积雨云。这些云塔可以堆积到18千米（11英里）高！积雨云也以雷雨云著称，因为它们通常会带来雷暴雨。

---

cumulonimbus *n.* 积雨云　　　　　　　　　　　　　thunderhead *n.* 雷雨云

20

Meteorologists Predict the Weather

Meteorologists are scientists who study the weather. They also make weather forecasts. They use tools to take weather data.

One tool that measures weather is a *radiosonde*. This is a small box on a weather balloon. First the balloon rises. Next the box records air pressure, temperature, and *humidity*. Then a radio sends the data back to a base.

气象学家对天气的预测

气象学家是研究天气的科学家。气象学家也能够预测天气。他们借助工具来获得有关天气的数据。

无线电高空测候仪就是他们预测天气时使用的工具之一。它是在气象气球上的一个小盒子。首先让气球升空，接下来小盒子就会监测空气压力、温度和湿度。然后通过无线电把数据传送给基地。

---

meteorologist *n.* 气象学家
humidity *n.* （空气中的）湿度

radiosonde *n.* 无线电高空测候器

Another tool is Doppler radar. A *radar* base sends out radio waves. The waves hit rain or snow and *bounce* back to the base. How long it takes the waves to bounce back tells how far away the rain or snow is. Radar can also read wind speed.

Weather satellites also provide data. They orbit Earth and send back photos of clouds. There are two kinds of weather satellites. One kind moves at a speed that keeps it above the same place on Earth. Another kind passes in a much lower orbit over different parts of Earth and provides more detailed photographs.

High-speed computers *compile* data from all of these tools. Meteorologists put the data together to make maps and *charts*. They know how the weather changes. They use the data and their knowledge to make forecasts.

　　另一个工具就是杜普勒雷达。雷达设备发送无线电波，电波碰撞到雨或是雪，然后反射回雷达。电波反射回来花费的时间就能告诉我们在多远的地方有雨或是雪。雷达也可以读出风速。

　　气象卫星也可以提供数据。它们绕地球轨道运行，能够发送回云层的图片。有两种气象卫星。一种是匀速气象卫星，它监测地球的同一位置。另一种就是在较低的轨道运行，经过地球的不同位置，提供更详细的图片。

　　高速运行的电脑汇编来自不同工具设备所采集的信息。气象科学家综合信息绘制地图气象图，由此了解了气象的变化，他们通过数据和他们的知识对天气进行预测。

---

radar *n.* 雷达　　　　　　　　　　　bounce *v.* （使）弹起；弹跳
compile *v.* 编译　　　　　　　　　　chart *n.* 图表

21

Fruits and Vegetables: A Key to Good Health

Each of us should eat five to nine *servings* of fruits and vegetables a day. In fact, one-third of all we eat should be fruits and vegetables. This may seem like a lot, but if you can do it your body will thank you.

Fruits and vegetables are plants. When we eat them, we get the energy that the

水果和蔬菜：身体健康的关键

我们每个人每天应该吃五到九份水果和蔬菜。事实上，我们每天吃的食物三分之一都应该是水果和蔬菜。这可能看起来会很多，但是如果你这样做，你的身体会感激你的。

水果和蔬菜都是植物，我们吃水果和蔬菜的时候，我们就能得到植物从太阳那获得的能量。植物中含有的水分可以减少我们的饥渴感。植物中

---

serving *n.* （供一个人吃的）一份食物的量

plants get from the sun. Plants contain water, which can make us less thirsty. They have fiber, which can help remove harmful materials from our bodies. Eating raw vegetables also can help keep our teeth clean.

Plant foods are high in *phytochemicals*. Phyto- means "plant." These plant chemicals work in many ways to help us stay healthy. They fight disease and make our bodies work better. Plants that have bright colors—such as red, green, and yellow—contain the most phytochemicals. Most orange vegetables contain beta *carotene*, which enables our bodies to produce vitamin A. Vitamin A is needed for good eyesight and healthy skin. Vitamin C is found in large amounts in oranges, melons, and *broccoli*. Vitamin C helps us grow blood *vessels*, bones, and teeth.

的纤维可以有助于移除我们身体中的有害物质。吃生菜有助于保持我们的牙齿清洁。

　　植物性食物含有较高的植物化学物质。"Phyto"代表着"植物"。这些植物通过多种方式的化学反应来帮助我们保持身体健康。它们能战胜疾病使我们的身体更加健康。有明亮颜色的植物，像红色、绿色和黄色，都富含植物化学物质。大部分橙色植物都富含能使身体合成维生素A的β-胡萝卜素。较好的视力和健康的皮肤都需要维生素A。维生素C大量存在于橘子、瓜和西兰花中。维生素C有助于血管、骨骼和牙齿的生长。为什

---

phytochemical *n.* 植物化学物质

broccoli *n.* 西兰花；绿菜花

carotene *n.* 胡萝卜素

vessel *n.* 血管；脉管

Why not just take vitamins in a pill? Most vitamin pills do not have as many kinds of vitamins as plants. Also, the vitamins in plants are easier for our bodies to use than the vitamins in pills are.

Unfortunately, most young people eat only one or two servings of fruits and vegetables a day. It is not difficult to add more fruits and vegetables to your diet. Put fruit on cereal for breakfast. *Munch* raw *veggies* at lunch instead of chips. A glass of real fruit juice instead of a soda is a healthful choice. Many fruits and vegetables make easy snacks. Eat a banana after school. Have a handful of grapes or an apple while doing homework. A salad with dinner and a slice of melon for dessert are other ways to get in the five to nine daily servings of fruits and vegetables.

么不直接吃维生素的药片呢？大多数的维生素药片没有植物中所含有的维生素种类多，而且，植物中的维生素比药片中的维生素更容易被人体消化吸收。

不幸的是大多数年轻人每天只吃一到两份水果和蔬菜。在日常饮食菜单中添加更多的水果和蔬菜并不是很困难。在谷类食物中添加一些水果作为早餐。中午，添加咀嚼性生蔬菜来代替薯条。用果汁来代替碳酸饮料也是一个不错的选择。很多水果和蔬菜可做成方便的零食。在放学后吃根香蕉，在做家庭作业的时候吃一串葡萄或是一个苹果，在晚饭时吃点沙拉，吃块瓜作为餐后甜点等很多种方法能使每天吃到五到九份水果和蔬菜。

---

munch *v.* 大声咀嚼；用力咀嚼　　　　　　　　　　veggie *n.* 蔬菜

A fruit or vegetable *smoothie* is a tasty dessert. You can cut up bananas, strawberries, or peaches and put them into a *blender*, along with a small amount of juice or milk. Frozen *yogurt* can be added for thickness. Both fruits and vegetables can be used to make smoothies as desserts. These can provide important nutrients while we enjoy the taste of delicious foods.

水果或是蔬菜的果汁是可口的甜点。你可以切些香蕉、草莓和桃，然后把它们放入搅拌机，添加一些果汁或牛奶。可以再添加一些冻酸奶来提高浓度。所有的水果和蔬菜都可以这样做成小甜点。这些能在我们品尝美味的同时为我们提供重要的营养物质。

smoothie *n.* 果汁；加奶（或冰淇淋）果汁　　　　blender *n.* （电动）食物搅拌器
yogurt *n.* 酸奶

22

Exotic Fruits

The word exotic means "from somewhere else," or "unusual." Some fruits are thought of as exotic. They include *kiwifruit*, *mangoes*, and *uniq* fruit.

Kiwifruit grows on vines in Asia, New Zealand, and California. This fruit is small and egg shaped, with a thin skin covered with brown *fuzz*. The inside of the fruit,

异国水果

"exotic"这个词意思是"来自其他地方的"或者是"不同寻常的"。有一些水果被认为是异国水果。其中有猕猴桃、芒果和牙买加丑橘。

猕猴桃生长在亚洲、新西兰和加利福尼亚州的藤本植物上。这种水果很小，蛋状，薄薄的果皮上有棕色的绒毛。水果的内部，叫做果肉，绿色

---

kiwifruit *n.* 猕猴桃；奇异果

uniq *n.* 柚橘

mango *n.* 芒果

fuzz *n.* 茸毛；绒毛

called the flesh, is green and juicy. It has small, dark purple seeds. Before eating a kiwifruit, remove the skin. Kiwifruit provides vitamins C and E.

Mangoes come in a variety of shapes and sizes. Often they are *oval* and about the size of an orange. The skin can be red, green, or yellow, and the flesh is orange. Mangoes grow on evergreen trees in warm areas of the world called the tropics. Mangoes first grew in India, so they are native to that country. Mangoes have vitamins A and C and are high in fiber. Remove the peel and the *pit* before eating a mango.

The uniq fruit was first found in Jamaica. It came from an accidental *cross* between a type of orange and a *grapefruit*. Uniq fruits are now grown in Florida. They are sometimes called Ugli fruit because of

---

而多汁。内部有小的、暗紫色的种子。在吃猕猴桃之前要把果皮去掉。猕猴桃提供丰富的维生素C和维生素E。

芒果有不同的形状和尺寸。通常芒果是椭圆形的橙子般大小。它的果皮有红色、绿色和黄色，果肉是橙色。芒果生长在热带地区的常青树木上，是典型的热带水果。芒果生长在印度，所以它们是印度的本土水果。芒果有丰富的纤维，也富含丰富的维生素A和维生素C。在吃芒果之前要去掉果皮和果核。

牙买加丑橘首先是在牙买加发现的。是一种橘子和葡萄柚意外杂交形成的水果。牙买加丑橘现在主要生长在佛罗里达州。它们有时被称为牙买

---

oval *adj.* 椭圆形的
cross *n.* 混合物；杂交品种

pit *n.* 果核
grapefruit *n.* 葡萄柚；西柚

their *puffy*, greenish-yellow skin. To eat one, peel it and eat it like an orange or cut it in half and eat it like a grapefruit. Like oranges, uniq fruits have lots of vitamin C.

加丑橘是因为它们庞大的体积和黄绿色的果皮。吃丑橘要像吃橙子那样剥掉果皮，或者像吃葡萄柚那样切成瓣。和橙子一样，牙买加丑橘富含丰富的维生素C。

puffy *adj.* 鼓胀的；肿胀的

23

Crossing the Land with Steam Power

At the end of the 18th century, land travel was slow and difficult. Most people did not travel far or very often. People might walk, ride a horse, or take a horse-drawn *carriage*. Farmers could not send their crops very far to market. Mail and goods took a long time to get from one place to another. Then people began to

使用蒸汽的力量横穿陆地

在18世纪末，陆上交通又慢又困难。大多数人不经常远行。人们可以步行、骑马或是乘坐马车。农民也不能把他们的农作物销往远处。邮件和货物从一个地方运送到另一个地方要花费很长时间。人们

carriage *n.* 四轮马车

build railroads for trains powered by steam *locomotives*. Steam power put people and goods on the move.

A steam engine changes steam energy to *mechanical* energy. Mechanical energy can be used to run engines and other types of machines. The first steam engine was very simple. Water in a *cylinder* was heated until it boiled. Boiling water changes to steam. Steam expands. The steam pushed up a machine part called a *piston*. As the cylinder cooled, it created suction that pulled the piston back down.

In 1705 a steam engine was made to run a pump in England. The pump drew water out of flooded mines. Then, in 1763, James Watt built a better steam engine. He developed it into one that used pistons to turn a wheel. It could power many types of machines that

---

开始为蒸汽火车修建铁路。蒸汽的力量能使人和货物移动起来。

蒸汽机使蒸汽能转化为机械能。机械能可以使发动机运转，也可以用在其他类型的机器上。第一台发动机的构造非常简单。水倒入气缸然后加热直到沸腾起来。沸腾的水转变为蒸汽，蒸汽扩张推动蒸汽机的活塞。当气缸冷却下来，它产生吸力，蒸汽又把活塞吸引回来。

1705年，在英格兰，蒸汽机被用来运行泵。泵用来抽出矿井中浸满的水。1763年，詹姆斯·瓦特发明了一台较好的蒸汽机，蒸汽机推动活

---

locomotive *n.* 机车；火车头
cylinder *n.* （发动机的）汽缸

mechanical *adj.* 机械的；机动的
piston *n.* 活塞

used *circular motion*.

Other English inventors made steam engines that could power *vehicles*. Richard Trevithick used a high-pressure steam engine to make the first steam locomotive. It pulled 10 tons of iron and 70 men on nine miles of track. It made just one trip, but that trip showed that steam power could pull *rail* cars. Later, in 1825, the first true railroad was in use in England. It carried people and goods on regular runs.

The first railroad in the United States was the Baltimore and Ohio (B&O). Horses had been pulling cars on a set of tracks. The tracks had sharp curves. The B&O wanted to try steam power, but English trains were too big for the tracks. Peter Cooper built a smaller train

---

塞使轮子转动。这种能量可以应用到其他类型的回转机器上。

其他的英国发明家用蒸汽机设计出了动力车。理查德·特里维西克用高功率的蒸汽机制造出第一台蒸汽发动机车。它可以运载10吨的铁和70个人运行9英里。这只是一次旅行，但它可以说明用蒸汽能可以拉动轨道车。后来，在1825年，第一条真正的铁路在英格兰投入使用。它可以在正常的行驶中运送人和物品。

美国的第一条铁路是在巴尔的摩和俄亥俄州。用马拉动铁轨上的车。铁轨有急弯曲线，所以巴尔的摩和俄亥俄州试着使用蒸汽机，但是英国的火车太大了，不适合这条铁轨。皮特·库珀制造了一个较小的火车，名叫

---

circular *adj.* 环形的；绕圈的　　　　　　motion *n.* 运动；移动
vehicle *n.* 交通工具；车辆　　　　　　　rail *n.* 铁轨；轨道

called the Tom Thumb. In 1830, the Tom Thumb made its first run. Ten years later, there were more than 2,000 miles of track in our country.

The railroads grew *rapidly*. By 1869 they ran all the way from the East Coast to the West Coast. People, goods, and mail moved quickly and safely. Steam power took them over the rails and across the land. Trips that once took weeks now took just two or three days.

大拇指汤姆。1830年，大拇指汤姆第一次试运。10年后，在美国就有超过2000英尺的铁轨。

铁路发展很迅速，到1869年火车能够从东海岸开到西海岸。人、货物和邮件都可以很迅速很安全的运送。蒸汽能把他们带入铁轨穿越各地。以前花费几个星期的旅行现在仅仅需要花费2到3天。

rapidly *adv.* 迅速地；快速地

24

Robert Fulton and the Steamboat

In the early 1700s, people had dreams of using steam to run boats. But they were just dreams. The first steam engines did not have enough power to run a boat. After James Watt built a better steam engine in 1763, the way was open for the dreams to become real.

A few inventors built early *steamboats*. In

罗伯特·富尔顿和蒸汽船

18世纪初，人们曾幻想把蒸汽机用到船上，但这仅仅是梦想。第一台蒸汽机没有足够的动力使船划动。1763年，詹姆斯·瓦特改进了蒸汽机以后，这个梦想逐渐成为现实。

有一些发明家发明建造了早期的蒸汽船。1786年，约翰·费奇建造

---

steamboat *n.* 汽船；轮船

1786, John Fitch built the first one in the United States. The boat had a steam engine that moved rows of *oars* through the water. It often broke down, however, and people did not take it very seriously.

Robert Fulton made the steamboat popular. Fulton was an American who went to London to study art. While he was there, he became *intrigued* by the study of mechanics. First he came up with a new kind of *canal* system and then a small steamboat. It traveled up the Seine River in France at 5 kilometers (3 miles) per hour.

Four years later, Fulton came back to the United States. President Jefferson wanted him to build canals, but Fulton wanted to build a new steamboat. His new boat had a flat bottom. There were *paddle*

了美国第一台蒸汽船。这个船有一个蒸汽机可以使一排排的浆划水。尽管它经常抛锚，但人们却不太在意。

罗伯特·富尔顿使蒸汽船流行了起来。富尔顿是美国人，去伦敦学习艺术。当他在伦敦时对学习机械产生了兴趣。首先他想出了一个新的运河体系，然后想到了一个小的蒸汽船。它可以在法国的塞纳河上以每小时5千米（3英里）的速度运行。

四年后，富尔顿回到了美国。杰弗逊总统想要他帮着修建运河，但是富尔顿想要建造一艘新的蒸汽船。新船是平底的，可以在两侧安装浆轮。

---

oar *n.* 船桨；桨
canal *n.* 运河

intrigued *adj.* 很感兴趣的；好奇的
paddle *n.* 桨；（机具的）桨状部分

wheels on each side. People called it Fulton's Folly. The boat's real name was the Clermont. In 1807, the Clermont went from New York City to Albany in just 32 hours. The same trip took an *average* of four days by *sailboat*. Soon steamboats were in use on many rivers.

人们称它是富尔顿的蠢物。这个船真正的名字是克莱蒙。1807年克莱蒙从纽约开往奥尔巴尼仅仅用了32小时。相同的旅程用帆船则平均得花四天的时间。很快蒸汽船就开始在很多条河流上使用。

average *n.* 平均数；平均水平   sailboat *n.* 帆船

25

Seasons Around the World

The seasons of the year are spring, summer, fall, and winter. They bring changes in temperature and weather. They also bring changes in the lengths of days. On summer days there are more hours of *daylight* than on winter days.

There are two reasons that the seasons and the hours of daylight change. The first

全球的季节

年有春夏秋冬四个季节。它们会带来温度和天气的变化。也会引起日照长短的变化。夏天的日照时间要比冬天长几个小时。

引起季节和日照长短变化的原因有两个。第一个就是地球绕太阳的公转。第二个原因就是倾斜的地轴。设想地球就是有一条直线通过其中心的

---

daylight *n.* 日光

is that Earth moves around the Sun, and the second is that the *axis* of Earth is *tilted*. Imagine Earth as a big ball with a line going through its middle. At the top of the line is the North Pole. At the bottom is the South Pole. The line is Earth's axis, on which it turns. Now imagine that the line is not straight up and down, but tilted.

Picture the tilted Earth as it moves around the Sun. Sometimes Earth's top half, which is called the Northern *Hemisphere*, is tilted toward the Sun. At the same time, the bottom half, or Southern Hemisphere, is tilted away from the Sun. At other times, the Southern Hemisphere is tilted toward the Sun, and the Northern Hemisphere is tilted away.

The half of Earth that is tilted toward the Sun gets more of the

---

大球。在这条直线的顶部是北极，底部是南极。这条直线就是地轴，地球绕着它转动。现在设想这条直线不是直上直下的，而是倾斜的。

设想倾斜的地球绕着太阳转动。有时，地区的上半部倾向太阳，这半球叫做北半球。与此同时，地球的下半部叫做南半球，背离太阳。有时南半球倾向太阳，北半球则背离太阳。

倾向太阳的那半球可以接收到更多的光和热。这半球就是夏天。背

---

axis *n.* 轴　　　　　　　　　　　　　　　　tilt *v.* （使）倾斜；倾侧
hemisphere *n.* （地球的）半球

Sun's light and heat. In this part of the world, it is summer. The half that is tilted away from the Sun gets less sunlight and heat. In this part of the world, it is winter. When it is summer in the United States, it is winter in Australia. The United States is in the Northern Hemisphere, and Australia is in the Southern Hemisphere.

The equator stays the same *distance* from the Sun all the time. The temperature stays the same, and the hours of daylight do not change. *Therefore*, there are no seasons. However, the amount of rain does change. Places on the equator have a wet season and a dry season.

What happens at the North and South Poles? The Sun shines all day at the start of summer. It is dark all day at the start of winter.

离太阳的那半球获得较少的光和热，这半球就是冬天。当美国是夏天的时候，澳大利亚则是冬天。美国在北半球，澳大利亚在南半球。

赤道距太阳的距离保持不变，所以赤道地区的温度和日照长短保持不变，从而没有季节的变化，然而降雨量是会发生变化的。在赤道地区有雨季和旱季之分。

在北极和南极会发生什么样的变化呢？在夏季会发生极昼，在冬季则会发生极夜。

distance *n.* 距离；间距　　　　　therefore *adv.* 因此；所以

Once a year, the Sun reaches its most northern point in the sky. This happens in June, and in the Northern Hemisphere it is called the summer *solstice*. This is the day with the most hours of daylight. In December, the Sun reaches its most southern point. This is our winter solstice, the day with the fewest hours of daylight.

一年中，太阳在空中到达最北端，这天会发生在六月，在北半球这天叫做夏至日，这天的日照时间最长。在十二月份太阳会到达最南端，这天我们叫做冬至日，这天的日照时间最短。

solstice *n.* 至（点）；（夏或冬）至

26

Staying Warm in Winter

Throughout history, people have found ways to keep warm during winter. Today we have both old ways and new ways of staying warm.

Down consists of the *fine*, soft feathers of a bird, such as a goose. The feathers *trap* air and slow down heat loss. Down has been used for hundreds of years in bed

冬季保暖

纵观历史，人们有不同的取暖方法。现在我们既有老式的又有新式的保暖方法。

鸟儿羽毛的组成既纤细又柔软，像鹅的羽毛，可以阻隔空气防止热量流失。铺盖在床上的东西叫被子，已经使用了数百年。现在有些人也还很喜欢鸭绒被、羽绒服和夹克。然而，现在有了一种新的保暖方法。人造合

---

fine *adj.* 纤细的；精致的   trap *v.* 收集；吸收

covers called *comforters*. Some people still like down comforters, coats, and jackets. Today, however, there is another choice. *Synthetic* down is made of *manufactured* fibers that work as well as feathers when dry and better than feathers when wet. The fibers are used in comforters and outdoor clothes.

Polar fleece is a new fabric made from recycled soda bottles. It is lightweight and warm. It keeps people dry by letting moisture pass through it and away from their bodies. Polar fleece is used for coats, jackets, hats, and gloves.

For cold fingers and toes, there are warmers that slip inside mittens or boots. These come sealed in a package. When the package is opened, the ingredients inside the warmers react to the air by heating up. Electric socks and mittens can also keep people warm. They have batteries that warm wires that run through the fabric.

成纤维在干的时候和羽绒一样保暖，在潮湿的时候要比羽绒更保暖。人造纤维常常用来做被子和户外服装。

摇粒绒是一种新型的织物，它是由回收的苏打水瓶做成的。质量很轻并且很保暖。它可以通过防止水分进入，保持干燥。摇粒绒可以用来做衣服，夹克，帽子和手套。

对于冷的手指和脚趾,有可以放进手套或靴子里的取暖器。取暖器是密封在一个包里的。当包裹被打开的时候,取暖器里面的成分通过加热和空气发生反应。电动袜子和手套也可以给人保暖，里面有电池,通过织物使电线变暖。

---

comforter *n.* 被子

manufactured *adj.* 人造的

synthetic *v.* 合成纤维（织物）

polar fleece 摇粒绒

27

What Is a Mammal?

Mammals are warm-blooded animals that produce milk to feed their young. Female mammals have *mammary glands*, which produce the milk. All mammals have *backbones* and hair. There are about 4,600 living species of mammals. The largest mammal is the blue whale. Blue whales can grow to be more than 33

哺乳动物

哺乳动物就是一种能够自产乳汁哺育幼子的恒温动物。雌性的哺乳动物都有乳腺，能够产生乳汁。所有的哺乳动物都有脊柱和毛发。现存的哺乳动物大约有4 600种。蓝鲸是最大的哺乳动物。蓝鲸能够长到33米（100英尺）多长。鼩鼱和老鼠是最小的哺乳动物，体长可以

---

mammary *adj.* 乳房的；乳腺的　　　　　　　　　　　gland *n.* 腺
backbone *n.* 脊柱

meters (100 feet) long. *Shrews* and mice are the smallest mammals. Some are less than 5 centimeters (2 inches) long.

Mammals live almost everywhere on Earth, including deserts, forests, grasslands, and mountains. Humans, rats, camels, skunks, lions, deer, and wolves are all mammals. You may have other mammals in your home. Dogs, cats, and hamsters are mammals.

Almost all mammals give birth to live young, but a few lay eggs. These mammals are called *monotremes*. Even though monotremes lay eggs, they still produce milk to feed their newly *hatched* young. There are only three kinds of monotremes. They are the *platypus* and two kinds of spiny anteaters.

Most mammals give birth to young that can live outside the

小于5厘米（2英寸）。

哺乳动物几乎遍布地球各个角落。包括沙漠、森林、草原和高山。人类、鼠类、骆驼、臭鼬、狮子、鹿和狼都是哺乳动物。你的家里也可能有其他的哺乳动物，像狗、猫、仓鼠等。

几乎所有的哺乳动物都能生育下一代，但也有一些产蛋。产蛋的哺乳动物叫做单孔目动物。单孔目动物虽然产蛋，但是它们也能够产生乳汁，哺育孵化出来的小生命。现在仅有三种单孔目哺乳动物，它们是鸭嘴兽和两种带刺的食蚁兽。

大多数新出生的小哺乳动物马上就可以在母体外面生存。也有一些哺

---

shrew *n.* 鼩鼱　　　　　　　　　monotreme *n.* 单孔目哺乳动物
hatch *v.* 孵化；孵出　　　　　　platypus *n.* 鸭嘴兽

mother's body right away. A few mammals have young that are born less mature. These mammals are called *marsupials*. Most marsupials live the first part of their lives in a *pouch* on their mother's body. Two kinds of marsupials are kangaroos and opossums.

Some mammals live in the water. These are called *aquatic* mammals, or sea mammals. Some people think that dolphins and whales are fish. They are not. They are sea mammals. Sea mammals have lungs for breathing. They must surface about every two minutes to breathe. Whales and dolphins breathe through a *blowhole* in the top of their heads. Some people think that whales and dolphins have no hair, but actually they do have a few hairs on their heads.

Another kind of sea mammal is the manatee, often called the

乳动物刚刚出生不成熟。这些哺乳动物叫做有袋类动物。大多数的有袋类动物出生后首先在它们母亲的育儿袋中生活一段时间。两种典型的有袋类动物就是袋鼠和负鼠。

有一些哺乳动物生活在水中，这些叫做水生哺乳动物或是海洋哺乳动物。一些人认为海豚和鲸是鱼类，但事实上它们不是鱼类，它们是海洋哺乳动物。海洋哺乳动物用肺呼吸。它们每隔两分钟就到水面上呼吸一次。鲸和海豚是通过头部的呼吸孔进行呼吸的。有人认为鲸和海豚没有毛发，但事实上它们有一些毛发在头部。

另一种海洋哺乳动物是海牛。经常被叫做"sea cow"。海牛是通过

---

marsupial *n.* 有袋类动物
aquatic *adj.* 水生的；水栖的

pouch *n.* （袋鼠等的）育儿袋
blowhole *n.* （鲸头顶的）呼吸孔

sea cow. Manatees breathe through snouts that they lift above the surface of the water. Seals and *walruses* are also sea mammals. So are polar bears. Polar bears spend a lot of time in the water hunting for food, such as seals and fish.

About one-fourth of mammal species are threatened. So few of these animals are left that they are in danger of dying out. Some of these species' habitats have been taken over by people. Some species have been poisoned by air and water *pollution*. Many have been hunted for food or for skins. Several groups are working to save these species.

游上水面用口鼻呼吸的。海豹和海象也是哺乳动物，北极熊也是哺乳动物。像海豹和鱼一样，北极熊大部分时间都是在水中寻找食物。

约有四分之一的哺乳动物面临威胁。有少部分的动物存活了下来处于濒临灭绝的状态。其中一些的栖息地已经被人类占用。有些物种已经中了空气污染和水污染的毒。人们为了食物和毛皮已经捕杀了很多动物。一些组织正致力于解救这些物种。

---

walrus *n.* 海象　　　　　　　　　　　　　pollution *n.* 污染；弄脏

28

Mammals with Pouches

Marsupials are one kind of mammal. Their young are born before they are fully formed. Most marsupials have a pouch where the young stay while they *develop*. While they grow in the pouch, the *newborns* feed on milk from the mother. When they are big enough, they leave the pouch to live on their own.

带有育儿袋的哺乳动物

有袋类动物是哺乳动物。他们的新生儿在还没发育完全之前就出生了。大部分的有袋类哺乳动物都有一个育儿袋。新生儿在育儿袋中成长。当它们在育儿袋中成长的时候，新生儿可以喝母乳。当它们长到足够大时，就离开育儿袋，开始独立的生活。有一些有袋类哺乳动物

---

develop *v.* （使）成长；发展   newborn *n.* 新生儿；婴儿

Some marsupials don't have a pouch. After birth, the young attach themselves to the mother. They stay attached until they can find food on their own.

Two well-known marsupials are kangaroos and *koalas*. Their young are called *joeys*. Kangaroos have pouches in front. A kangaroo joey may stay in the pouch for as long as six months. Koalas look like small bears, and they climb trees. A koala's pouch is on its back. A koala joey also may stay in the pouch for up to six months. It might ride on its mother's back for six more months.

There are many other kinds of marsupials. Some, such as *marsupial mice*, are very small. Others, such as *wombats*, are larger. Wombats are short animals with thick fur. A wombat can be 1 meter

---

没有育儿袋。它们出生后就依附在母亲身上。直到它们可以自己捕食。

两种著名的有袋类哺乳动物是袋鼠和考拉。它们很小的时候被叫做幼袋鼠。袋鼠在前面有一个育儿袋。小袋鼠在育儿袋中可待到6个月。考拉看起来很像小熊。它们爬树。考拉的育儿袋在背部。小考拉也在育儿袋中待6个月，也可以在母亲后背待6个月以上。

也有一些其他的带有育儿袋的哺乳动物。有些非常小，像是袋鼬。另一些大的，像是袋熊。袋熊是一种有厚毛皮的矮小动物。小袋熊大约有1米长（3.25英尺）。重量可达16千克（35磅）。袋熊生活在地洞中。他们

---

koala *n.* 考拉；树袋熊
marsupial mouse 袋鼬

joey *n.* 幼袋鼠；幼负鼠
wombat *n.* 毛鼻袋熊

(3¼ feet) long and weigh 16 kilograms (35 pounds). Wombats live in the ground in *burrows*. They eat roots and grass. They are *nocturnal*; that is, they sleep during the day. *Tasmanian devils* weigh about 9 kilograms (20 pounds) and have long tails and pointed snouts. They eat dead animals. They also hunt and kill small animals for food.

吃草和树根。它们是白天睡觉的夜行动物。袋獾重大约9千克（20磅），有长长的尾巴和突出的口鼻部。它们以死掉的动物为食。它们也捕食一些小动物作为食物。

---

burrow *n.* （动物的）洞穴；地道   nocturnal *adj.* 夜间活动的
tasmanian devil 袋獾

29

How to Organize a Great Science Fair Project

How can you create a great *science fair project*? You can start by asking yourself the following questions.

(1) What interests me? You can connect almost any topic to science. Your topic could be plants, worms, dogs, the sky, or something else. If you can't think of a topic, look in books or on the Internet. Ask a

怎样安排一次重要的科学展示项目？

怎样创建一个重要的科学项目？你可以通过问自己这些问题来开始。

（1）什么使我感兴趣？你可以把任何题目和科学联系起来。你的课题可以是植物、虫子、狗、天空或其他的事物。如果你想不出课题，在课本或网上寻找，找图书馆管理员或老师寻求帮助。你的父母也许有一些好

---

science fair project *n.* 科学项目

librarian or your teacher for help. Your parents may have some good ideas.

(2) What question do I have about this topic? A great science project always includes an experiment. Make sure that your question can be answered by doing an experiment. Here are some examples of questions. Does the amount of light have an effect on how fast plants grow? How much salt is in different kinds of cookies sold at the store? Why does the sky change color at different times of the day?

(3) How much time do I have before the science fair? If the science fair is in two weeks, you won't have time for some types of experiments, such as growing plants. Carefully plan your project so that you have enough time to do your experiment *accurately*.

的想法。

（2）关于这个课题我有什么问题？一个好的科研项目总要包括实验。要确保你的问题可以通过实验得到解决。这里有一些问题的例子，光的照射量对植物生长快慢有影响吗？商店里出售的不同种类的曲奇饼中食用盐的量是多少？为什么天空在一天中的不同时间会改变颜色？

（3）在一项科学展示之前我有多少时间？如果科研展示是在两周之内，你就不会有时间进行一些类型的实验，例如，种植物。仔细地计划你的项目，这样你会有足够的时间准确地完成实验。

---

accurately *adv.* 正确无误地；准确地

(4) What do I think is the answer to my question? Why do I think this? This is your hypothesis, or *explanation*. You will prove it right or wrong by doing an experiment. Let's look at the sky question. Your hypothesis might be "The color of the sky is related to the position of the sun."

(5) How can I prove my hypothesis? This is where the experiment comes in. You have to test your hypothesis. If you were trying to find out about how light affects plant growth, you could plant seeds in a number of *containers*. Then you could expose them to different amounts of light.

(6) How can I record my experiment? For the plant experiment, you might measure each plant once a week and write the data on a chart. You could take pictures of the plants each week.

（4）我要考虑我的问题的答案是什么？为什么我要考虑它？这是你的假设或解释。你可以通过实验证明它的对与错。让我们来看一下天空的问题。你的假设可能是"天空的颜色和太阳的位置有关。"

（5）我怎么样证明我的假设？这就是进行实验的切入点。你不得不测试你的假设。如果你想知道光是怎么样影响植物生长的，你应该在一些容器中种上种子。然后把它们暴露在不同的光强下。

（6）我怎么样记录我的实验？对植物的实验来说，你可以每周测量一次植物，把数据记录在表格上。你可以每周给植物拍照片。

---

explanation *n.* 解释；说明   container *n.* 容器

(7) How can I present my results? You might use *poster* board to show your question and hypothesis. You might add pictures and *graphs*. A great science project also states a conclusion. This might be "The plants that got the most light grew the fastest."

When you are done with your project, you may have more questions. A great science project makes you want to learn even more.

（7）我怎样展示我的结果？你可以用海报展示你的问题和假设。你可以加入图片和图表。一项大的科学研究也要说明结论。这可能是"阳光最充足的时候，植物生长得最快。"

当项目进行时，你可能会有更多的问题。一项大的科学研究会促使你学到很多的知识。

---

poster *n.* 招贴画；海报   graph *n.* 图表；曲线图

30

A Tasteful Science Experiment

Where on our tongues do we taste *bitter*, sweet, salty, and *sour* flavors? Here's an experiment to find the answer. You will need sugar, *lemon* juice, salt, instant coffee, a cookie sheet, and a small bowl.

On the cookie sheet, make tiny piles of sugar, salt, and coffee *grains*. Next, pour a

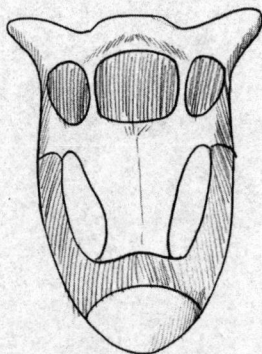

一次美味的科研实验

在我们舌头上的什么部位会尝到苦的、甜的、咸的和酸的味道？这有一项实验可以找到答案。你需要糖、柠檬汁、盐、即溶咖啡、甜面包片和一个小碗。

在面包片上，涂上少量的糖、盐和咖啡粒。接下来，在小碗中倒几滴柠檬汁。然后，浸湿你的手指，在糖中沾一下，放在舌头的中间位置停留

---

bitter *adj.* 味苦的　　　　　　　　　　　sour *adj.* 酸的
lemon *n.* 柠檬　　　　　　　　　　　　　grain *n.* 颗粒；细粒

few drops of lemon juice into the bowl. Then, wet your finger, dip it in the sugar and hold it against the center of your tongue. What do you taste? Now press the sugar on the front of your tongue and see if the taste varies.

Next, *rinse* out your mouth with water. *Dip* your finger into the salt and press it against the center of your tongue. Then press it on your tongue near one side and see how it tastes different.

Now rinse your mouth and try the coffee on the center of your tongue. Then try it on the back of your tongue. Rinse your mouth again. Finally, try the lemon juice in the center of your tongue, and then near the side of your tongue.

What did you learn? The center of your tongue does not taste things very well. The front of your tongue tastes sweet things, and the sides taste salty and sour things. The back of the tongue tastes bitter things.

一会。你尝到了什么？现在把糖放在舌头的前面，感觉味道是否有变化。

下一步，用水漱口。用手指沾上盐放在舌头的中心位置。然后再放在舌头侧边，感觉味道怎么变化。

再漱口，试着把咖啡放在舌头的中心位置。然后再在舌头的后面试一试。再次漱口。最后，用柠檬汁在舌头的中心试一下，然后在舌头边上试一下。

你了解到了什么？舌头的中心部分尝东西不是很好。舌头的前面会尝到甜的东西，舌头的边上尝咸的和酸的东西。舌头的后边尝苦的东西。

---

rinse *v.* （用清水）冲掉；冲洗　　　　　　　　　　dip *v.* 蘸；浸

31

Rocks and Minerals

If you hold a rock in your hands, you are holding a piece of our planet. Earth is basically made of rock. Rock is a mass of *mineral deposits*. All things in nature that are not animals or plants are minerals. Some minerals, such as salt, coal, and gold, are solid. Other minerals, such as water and natural gas, are not solid.

岩石和矿物质

如果你手里有一块岩石，那么你就拥有我们的地球一小部分了。地球基本上是由岩石组成的。岩石是大块的矿床。自然界中除了动物和植物所有物质都是矿物质。一些矿物质，如盐、煤和金子是固体。其他的矿物质，如水、自然中的气体不是固体。

---

mineral *n.* 矿物；矿物质　　　　　　　deposit *n.* （地下自然形成的）
　　　　　　　　　　　　　　　　　　　　　　　　　　　　沉积物；沉积层

A geologist is a scientist who studies what Earth is made of and how it was formed. Geologists classify rocks in groups. The names of the groups *indicate* how the rock was made. *Igneous* rock is formed as hot magma cools. Igneous means "fire-formed." Magma is melted rock that comes from deep within Earth, where the temperature is extremely high. Magma can harden and form rock if it rises to the surface of Earth. *Granite* is formed this way. When magma rises to the surface in a volcano, it is called lava. Rocks formed from lava are called *basalts*. These are the most common kinds of igneous rocks.

Sedimentary rock forms when layers of hard minerals blend together. This can happen over time or from the force of water or wind. Two common kinds of sedimentary rocks are sandstone and

---

地质学家是研究地球是由什么组成并且它是怎么形成的科学家。地质学家把岩石分成很多种。通过名称就表明了岩石是怎么形成的。火成岩是由热的岩浆冷却形成的。火成的意思是"火形成的"。岩浆是由地球深处的岩石融化形成的,地球内部的温度相当高。岩浆如果到地表面就会硬化形成岩石。花岗岩就是这样形成的。当岩浆到达地表面而存在火山中时,它被叫做火山熔岩。从火山熔岩中形成的岩石叫玄武岩。这些都是火成岩最普遍的种类。

当坚硬的矿物质层层混合在一起就形成了沉积岩。这需要经过很长时

---

indicate *v.* 表明;显示
granite *n.* 花岗岩;花岗石

igneous *adj.* 火成的
basalt *n.* 玄武岩

limestone. If you look closely at these rocks, you can see the layers.

When igneous or sedimentary rock is *subjected* to strong heat and pressure, it may turn into *metamorphic* rock. Metamorphic rock is made up of rock that has changed its form. One example is marble, which has many colors and is harder than the rocks from which it is made.

Geologists also separate rocks into groups based on how the rocks look. They call some minerals crystals. Diamonds are crystals that are made from a mineral called carbon. They are the hardest things on Earth. *Graphite* is pure carbon, too, but it is very soft. Graphite is used to make pencil lead. The difference in hardness is due to the amount of heat and pressure put on the carbon. Graphite

间或借助水或风的力量才能形成。两种普遍的沉积岩是砂岩和石灰石。如果你仔细观察这些岩石，就能看见分层。

当火成岩或沉积岩遇到强烈的撞击或巨大的压力时，它们可能转变成变质岩。变质岩是由已经变化的岩石组成的。一个例子就是大理石，它有许多颜色，并且要比组成它的岩石要硬。

地质学家也根据岩石的外观而把岩石分类。他们叫某种矿物水晶。钻石是由一种叫做碳的矿物质组成的晶体。它们是地球上最硬的物质。石墨也是纯净的碳，但是它非常软。石墨经常用来做铅笔芯。它们硬度上的不

limestone *n.* 石灰岩
metamorphic *adj.* 变质的；变性的

subject *v.* 使臣服；使顺从
graphite *n.* 石墨

is not the only soft mineral. Another is talc, which is ground up to make *talcum powder*.

Geologists refer to some minerals as metals. Iron is a metal. Most of the iron we use comes from the mineral *hematite*. This rock is red, or black with red *streaks*. The streaks are the iron. They are red because iron rusts when it is exposed to air and water.

同是由于加在碳上的热和压力不同。石墨不是唯一软的矿物质。另外一种是滑石，它被研磨用来做滑石粉。

地质学也涉及到一些金属矿物质。铁是一种金属，我们使用的大多数铁都来自于赤铁矿。这种岩石是红色的，或者是黑色的带有红色的条纹。这些红色的条纹就是铁。当铁暴露在空气和水中的时候会生锈，因此它们是红色的。

---

talcum powder *n.* 滑石粉；爽身粉   hematite *n.* 赤铁矿
streak *n.* 条纹；条痕

32

The Hope Diamond

The Hope diamond is a rare and famous *gem*. It has a complex history. In the 1600s, a French traveler bought a blue diamond the size of a *fist*. It most likely came from India. He sold the stone to the French king in 1668. The stone was recut and worn on a *ribbon*. When a diamond is recut, a jeweler cuts off pieces

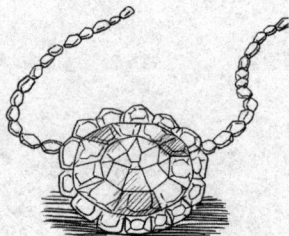

希望之星

希望之星钻石是一块非常著名的稀有的宝石。它有一段很复杂的历史。在17世纪时，一个法国的旅行家买了一块拳头大小的蓝宝石。它很有可能是来自印度。在1668年的时候，他把宝石卖给了法国的国王。这块宝石被重新切割并被镶嵌在了绶带上。当一块钻石被切割时，珠宝商会让它更光亮并且有不同的形状。这块重新切割的钻石被叫做

gem *n.* 宝石　　　　　　　　　　　　　　　　fist *n.* 拳；拳头
ribbon *n.* 绶带；勋带

to make it shinier and give it a different shape. The recut diamond was named the French Blue. During the French *Revolution*, it *vanished* and no one knew who had it.

In 1812 it was reported that a London diamond seller had a large blue diamond. Many experts believe that it was the French Blue and that it had been recut. Later, King George IV of England owned the diamond. It was sold after he died.

By 1839 the stone belonged to Henry Philip Hope, a London banker. While Hope had the gem, it was named the Hope diamond. After Hope died, members of his family sold it to pay debts.

The next owner took it to Paris. It was sold and then resold to Pierre Cartier, a famous jeweler. He sold it to Evalyn Walsh McLean,

---

"法国之蓝"。在法国大革命期间，它消失了，没有人知道谁拥有它。

据报道，在1812年，一位伦敦的珠宝商有一块大的蓝宝石。许多专家都相信那就是法国之蓝，并且被重新切割了。后来，英国的国王乔治四世拥有了它。在他死后，蓝钻石被卖掉了。

直到1839年，这颗钻石属于一位伦敦的银行家亨利·菲利浦·侯普。由于是侯普拥有它，因此这颗钻石得名"希望"。侯普去世之后，他的家人把钻石卖了还债。

下一个拥有者把它带到了巴黎。它被卖了，然后又被转卖给了著名的

---

revolution *n.* 革命   vanish *v.* （莫名其妙地）突然消失

a wealthy woman in Washington, D.C. She later had it set in a *necklace*. After she died, a jeweler named Harry Winston bought the diamond. Years later, he gave it to the Smithsonian *Institution* in Washington, D.C. It is there now for all to see.

珠宝商皮埃尔·卡蒂尔。他把它卖给了华盛顿一位富有的夫人艾芙琳·沃尔什·麦克林。随后她把它镶在项链里。她死后，一位叫哈利·温斯顿的珠宝商买下了这颗钻石。多年之后，他把这颗钻石送给了在华盛顿的史密森尼博物院。在那里所有的人都可以看到它。

necklace *n.* 项链　　　　　institution *n.* （大学、银行等规模大的）机构

33

How Cacti Survive with Little Water

Deserts are very dry places because they get so little rain. Yet plants do grow there. The *cactus* is one plant that has adapted to life with very little water. These plants have thick *stems* that can store large amounts of water. Some cacti have very tall stems. Others have stems that are round and shaped almost like a *barrel*.

仙人掌怎么能在几乎没有水的条件下生存？

沙漠中几乎很少下雨，所以沙漠是非常干燥的地方。然而植物却可以在那里生存。仙人掌就是一种能在水很少的条件下生存的植物。这些植物有很厚的茎能存留住许多的水分。一些仙人掌有很高的茎。其他也有一些仙人掌的茎是圆的，形状就像桶一样。

---

cactus *n.* 仙人掌　　　　　　　　　　　　　stem *n.* （花草的）茎
barrel *n.* 桶

The skin of the cactus has a *waxy coating*. This helps the plant hold in moisture. The stems of tall cacti have *ribs* that run from the top to the bottom. While the cacti are holding a lot of water, the stem is *swollen* and the ribs flatten out. As the stem loses water and shrinks, the ribs stand out more and more. Then the ribs help shade the stem and hold it up during the times that it is smaller. When the stem loses much of its water, it may bend. This shades part of the plant and helps keep it from losing more water.

Cacti have very small leaves or no leaves at all. They do have spines. These help shade the stem and can direct rainwater down to the roots. Cactus roots are near the surface. They spread out over a wide area. This allows them to absorb more water from rainfall. For this reason, cacti are spaced far apart.

　　仙人掌的表面有一层蜡质。这帮助植物保持一定的水分。高柱状的仙人掌的茎有从顶部到底部的叶肋。由于仙人掌要锁住大量的水分，它的茎很肥厚，叶肋变得扁平。由于茎失去水分而萎缩，叶肋就变得越来越突出。这样，在茎比较小的时候叶肋帮忙撑住了它。当茎失去大部分的水分时，它会变弯，遮住了植物的大部分，使它不流失更多的水分。

　　仙人掌的叶子很小，甚至没有叶子。它们有刺。这帮助遮挡住茎并且能直接把雨水送往根部。仙人掌的根接近地表面。它们延伸到很远的地方。这使得它们可以从降水中吸收更多的水分。正是这个原因，仙人掌分布在很广的地方。

---

waxy *adj.* 蜡制的；似蜡的　　　　　　coating *n.* （薄的）覆盖层
rib *n.* 肋骨　　　　　　　　　　　　swollen *adj.* 肿胀的；肿起来的

34

Flowering and Nonflowering Plants

People grow flowers in order to enjoy their beauty. Flowers are nice to look at, but they have another purpose. Flowers make seeds that can grow into new plants. Plants that have flowers are called *angiosperms*.

A flower has four parts that are arranged around a center. The outer part is a circle

开花植物和不开花植物

人们种花是为了欣赏它们的美丽。花很好看，但是它们有另外的作用。花的种子可以种到新的土地上。开花的植物叫做被子植物。

花的中心排列有四部分。最外面的部分是由萼片组成一轮花萼。通常

---

angiosperm *n.* 被子植物

made up of *sepals*. These are usually green and look like a ring of leaves. Sometimes they form a cup. The next part of a flower is a circle made of *petals*. They are larger than the sepals. Petals are the part of the flower you notice first. This is because they are usually white or a bright color. Petals come in many different shapes and sizes. Some petals are single and others are connected to one another.

In the middle of the petals are the *stamens*, which are thin and bend easily. They produce *pollen*. At the very center of the flower are the carpels. The seeds are produced here. For seeds to grow, pollen from the stamens must first enter the carpels. This process is called pollination.

为绿色，并且看上去像一圈叶子。有时它们形成杯子形状。另一部分是由花瓣组成的一圈。它们比萼片大。花瓣是你最先看到的部分。这是因为它通常是白色或是亮的颜色。花瓣有很多的不同的形状和大小。一些花瓣是单独的，另一些是和其他的连着的。

在花瓣的中心是雄蕊，雄蕊很细并且很易弯曲。它产生花粉。在一朵花的正中心是心皮。种子是在这里产生的。由于种子要长大，雄蕊产生的花粉必须首先进入到心皮中。这个过程叫授粉。

---

sepal *n.* 萼片　　　　　　　　　　　　petal *n.* 花瓣
stamen *n.* 雄蕊　　　　　　　　　　　pollen *n.* 花粉

Some plants don't flower at all yet still produce seeds. They are called *gymnosperms*, which means "naked seeds." Their seeds do not grow in carpels. Instead, the seeds grow in cones, such as pinecones. Some gymnosperms are short plants, and others are tall trees. Besides pine trees, gymnosperms also include fir trees and redwoods.

Another group of nonflowering plants, called *tracheophytes*, does not produce any seeds at all. Instead, these plants produce tiny objects called *spores*. Tracheophytes include *ferns*. It may look as if ferns have long branches with short leaves. These branches are actually called fronds. On the underside of a fern frond are small brown bumps, called sori. The sori protect cell cases where

---

　一些植物根本没有花但是仍然有种子。它们叫做裸子植物，意思是"裸露的种子"。它们的种子不长在雌蕊里。相反它们的种子生长在果实里，如松果。一些裸子植物是矮小的植物，另外的一些是高大的树木。除了松树，裸子植物还包括冷杉树和红杉。

　另外一种无花的植物叫做维管植物，它根本不产生种子。相反，这些植物产生一种微小的物质叫做孢子。维管植物包括蕨类植物。维管植物可能看上去像蕨类植物长了长的枝干和很短的叶子。这些枝干实际上叫做叶状体。在蕨类植物的叶状体的底部有小的褐色的凸起，叫做芽孢囊群。这

---

gymnosperm　*n.* 裸子植物　　　　　tracheophyte　*n.* 维管植物；导管植物
spore　*n.* 孢子　　　　　　　　　fern　*n.* 蕨；蕨类植物

cells grow into spores. When it is warm, the cell cases dry out and break open. The spores are then carried away by the wind. A spore that lands where there is the right amount of heat and moisture can grow into a fern.

Mosses are part of a group of nonflowering plants called *bryophytes*. These plants lack roots, stems, and leaves. They are not able to *transport* water and nutrients within themselves. Each part of the plant must absorb its own water and nutrients. Most bryophytes live in wet and shady locations. Like ferns, mosses have spores rather than seeds.

些芽孢囊群保护合子，合子是细胞分裂成孢子的地方。当环境温暖时，合子会变干破裂。然后孢子会被风吹走。孢子落在温度和湿度都适宜的地方就能生长成蕨类植物。

　　苔藓是无花植物类中的一种，叫做苔藓植物。这些植物没有根、茎、叶。它们自己不能运输水和营养。植物的每一部分都必须自己吸收水分和营养。大多数苔藓植物都生活在潮湿和背阴的地方。像蕨类植物一样，苔藓有孢子而没有种子。

bryophyte *n.* 苔藓植物   transport *v.* 运输；输送

35

The Honeybee and Pollination

Flowers have special glands between their petals. A gland is an organ that produces a *liquid*. The glands between petals make a sweet liquid known as *nectar*.

Honeybees use nectar to make honey. They use honey for food. A bee flies from one flower to the next to collect nectar. It

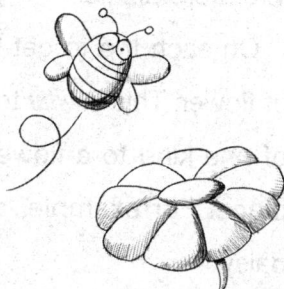

蜜蜂和授粉

花在花瓣之间有特殊的腺体。腺体就是产生液体的一个器官。从花瓣中产生的一种甜的液体叫做花蜜。

蜜蜂用花蜜去生产蜂蜜。它们把蜂蜜当做食物。蜜蜂从一朵花飞到另一朵花上去采花蜜。它把花蜜储存在接近肚子的一个小囊中，在这里把花

---

liquid *n.* 液体

nectar *n.* 花蜜

stores the nectar in a tiny *sac*, near its stomach, where the nectar turns into honey. At the same time that the bee takes in nectar, pollen from the stamens of the flower sticks to its legs. When the bee lands on another flower to get more nectar, some of the pollen on its legs *rubs* off on the plant's carpel. The carpel contains *ovules*, where eggs are formed. Pollination happens when pollen combines with an egg to form a seed. Seeds can drop from the plant and grow into more plants.

On each trip to get honey, a bee will usually go to the same type of flower. This is *vital* to the flowers. If the bee flew only from a flower of one kind to a flower of another kind, pollination would not take place. For example, a rose can't form a seed with pollen from a daisy.

One bee can visit up to 300 flowers in an hour. Now you know why bees are busy!

蜜变成蜂蜜。与此同时，蜜蜂采集花蜜时，花的雄蕊中花粉会粘在它的腿上。当蜜蜂到下一朵花上采集花蜜时，它腿上的一些花粉就会落在植物的心皮上。心皮包含胚珠，胚珠是卵子形成的地方。当花粉和卵子结合形成种子的时候就发生了授粉。种子会从植物中脱落长成更多的植物。

当蜜蜂采集蜂蜜的时候，它通常都会去同一种类型的花上。这对花来说很重要。如果蜜蜂只是从一种花飞到另一种花上，那么就不会发生授粉。比如说，玫瑰不可能和雏菊的花粉形成种子。

一只蜜蜂在一个小时之内能到过多达300朵花。现在你知道为什么蜜蜂这么忙了吧！

---

sac *n.* （动物体内的）囊
ovule *n.* 胚珠；卵细胞

rub *v.* 擦；磨
vital *adj.* 对……极重要的

36

Waste and Recycling

Each year, people in the United States throw out more than 220 million tons of garbage. That's an average of about 2 kilograms (4½ pounds) per person each day. Figuring out what to do with so much waste is a huge problem. Most of the waste goes to *landfills*, where it is buried. This gets rid of the trash but can

废物与回收

在美国，人们每年都会扔掉2.2亿多吨的垃圾。那就是相当于每人每天扔掉两公斤的垃圾。怎么样处理这些垃圾是一个巨大的难题。大多数的垃圾都送去了处理垃圾的地方——垃圾填埋厂。这样虽然摆脱了垃圾但是可能会产生更大的问题。垃圾填埋厂可能会泄露化学物质而

---

landfill *n.* 废物埋填地（或场）

create other problems. Landfills can leak chemicals that pollute the land and water. Our landfills are filling up fast, and in some parts of the country we are running out of places for new ones.

Not all of our waste goes into landfills. Some of it is burned in big *furnaces* called *incinerators*. This can pollute the air. The rest of our waste gets recycled. To recycle means to make new things out of used things.

Paper is one of the easiest materials to recycle. Some kinds of paper that are recycled are newspaper, *cardboard*, and paper that is used in offices. When newspaper is recycled, it is mixed with hot water and turned into pulp. The pulp is mixed with a chemical that removes ink. The pulp is then used to make new paper. Recycled

---

污染土地和水。我们的垃圾填埋厂填充的速度很快，并且在国家的一些地区，我们正在找新的地方建新的填埋厂。

并不是所有的垃圾都送去垃圾填埋厂。一些垃圾会被送到叫做焚烧炉的大炉子里燃烧。这会污染空气。其余的垃圾会得到回收。回收意味着从旧的东西中得到新的东西。

纸是最简单的回收材料的一种。回收的一些纸的种类有报纸、硬纸板，还有办公室中使用的纸。纸在回收时，它和烫的水混合然后变成纸浆。纸浆和一种除去墨的化学物质混合。然后纸浆用来做新的纸。回收的

---

furnace *n.* 熔炉；锅炉　　　　　　　　incinerator *n.* （焚烧垃圾的）焚化炉
cardboard *n.* 硬纸板；卡纸板

paper is much less expensive to make than new paper is.

About two-thirds of all steel is recycled. Some *scrap* steel is melted in a furnace and made into sheets. The sheets are used in making new cars, cans, and *appliances*.

About two-thirds of *aluminum beverage* cans are reused. The cans are crushed, then shredded and melted. Then they are made into large sheets. New cans are shaped from the sheets.

About a third of all glass is recycled. Almost all of this is from used glass containers. The glass is sorted by color into clear, brown, and green. It is melted and then formed into new glass items.

A small amount of plastic is reused. Plastic is harder to recycle than paper, steel, or glass. There are seven kinds of plastic used for

---

纸的制作成本要比新纸低得多。

大约三分之二的钢材被回收。一些钢的碎料在炉中被融化然后制成片状。这些钢片用来制造新的汽车、容器和家电等。

大约三分之二的铝制饮料罐被重新利用。这些罐子被粉碎，然后被切碎融化。最后它们被制成大的铝片。这些铝片被制成新的罐。

大约三分之一的玻璃被回收。几乎所有的这些都来自用过的玻璃容器。玻璃按颜色分为透明的、褐色的和绿色的。它们被融化然后形成新的玻璃制品。

一小部分的塑料被重新利用。塑料要比纸、钢、玻璃更难回收。有七

---

scrap *n.* 碎片；小块
aluminum *n.* 铝

appliance *n.* （家用）电器；器具
beverage *n.* （除水以外的）饮料

containers. Each kind must be recycled separately. A number on the bottom of each plastic item tells what kind of plastic it is made of. Used plastic can be cleaned, shredded into *flakes*, and then *melted* into *bits*. These bits can be used to make new things.

Recycling is a good way to get rid of waste. Researchers are constantly looking for new, less expensive ways to recycle.

种塑料被用作容器。每一种都必须单独回收。每一种塑料品底部的数字都说明了这是由哪种塑料制成的。用过的塑料品可以被清洗，切碎成片，然后融化成小片。这些小片可以用来制作新的东西。

回收是一种避免浪费的好方式。研究人员正在不断地寻找新的，更廉价的回收方法。

---

flake *n.* 小薄片；碎片   melt *v.* （使）熔化；（使）融化
bit *n.* 小量；小块

37

Our Class Recycling Project

Our science class did a recycling project. Our teacher, Mr. Akerede, divided the class into three teams. Each team worked on one activity. My friend Cole was on the waste-exchange team. Members planned a kind of free *garage sale*. People brought things they no longer wanted or used, and they placed them on

课堂上的有关回收的课题

在我们的科学课上做了一个回收的任务。我们的老师阿克瑞得先生把学生分成三组。每一组都有一个活动。我的朋友卡尔在废品交换组。组员设计一种自由的旧物销售模式。人们拿来他们不想要或再也用不上的东西，并把它们放到桌子上。任何拿东西来交换的人可以拿走

---

garage sale （在私人住宅的车库里进行的）旧物销售

tables. Anyone who brought something to the exchange could take anything he or she could use. My mother traded a rake for a *hammer*.

I was *captain* of the No Trash Challenge Day. Our class challenged Ms. Johnson's class to see which group could get through a school day with the smallest amount of trash. My team took away all the *wastebaskets* and gave everyone a plastic bag to carry. All trash had to go into the bags. At the end of the day, we compared our class pile with the pile from Ms. Johnson's class. Our class won! My class had waste-free lunches. We brought our lunches in reusable containers instead of paper bags. We brought apples and oranges instead of candy bars with wrappers. We put the orange peels and apple cores on the school *compost* heap.

The news team made posters for the No Trash Challenge. They sent information on the waste exchange to the local newspaper. They wrote a newsletter to tell people how to recycle more.

他或她可能用得上的物品。我母亲用一把耙子换了一把锤子。

　　我是"挑战无垃圾日"队的队长。我们班挑战约翰逊老师的班级，看哪一组可以在学校度过一天，并让垃圾量最少。我们组拿走了所有的废纸篓，同时给每个人一个塑料袋去装垃圾。所有的垃圾都要扔到袋中。一天结束之后，把我们班堆积的垃圾和约翰逊老师的班级堆积的垃圾相比较。结果是我们班胜利了！我们班没有浪费的午餐。我们用可重复使用容器带午餐而不是用纸袋。我们带苹果和橘子而不带有包装的糖果。我们把橘子皮和苹果核扔在学校的肥料堆上。

　　新闻组为"挑战无垃圾"制作了海报。他们把废品交换的信息发给当地报纸。他们写了简讯告诉人们怎样回收更多的东西。

---

hammer *n.* 锤子；榔头
wastebasket *n.* 废纸篓；废纸箱

captain *n.* 领导者；队长
compost *n.* 混合肥料；堆肥

38

Elijah McCoy, Inventor

Some people are curious about how mechanical things work. They have *creative* minds and like to build new things. They might watch someone do a job and think up a way to make the job easier or safer. These people are known as inventors.

Elijah McCoy was an inventor. His parents had been *slaves* in Kentucky. They ran away to Canada so they could be free.

发明家以利亚·麦科伊

　　一些人对机械类的东西是怎么工作的很感兴趣。他们有创造性的想法并喜欢制造新的东西。他们可能观察一个人工作，然后想出一种使这个工作更简便或更安全的方法。这类人被认为是发明家。

　　以利亚·麦科伊是一位发明家。他的父母曾是肯塔基州的奴隶。他们为了自由逃到加拿大。麦科伊于1844年出生在安大略省。他直到15岁那年才

creative *adj.* 创造性的　　　　　　　　　　　　　　　　slave *n.* 奴隶

McCoy was born in Ontario in 1844. He went to school there until he was 15 years old. He was very interested in how mechanical things worked. His parents sent him to a school in Scotland. There he learned to be a mechanical engineer. Mechanical engineers design machines.

While McCoy was in Scotland, the *Civil War* was being fought in the United States. After the war, McCoy went home to Canada. Soon he moved to Michigan and got a job on a railroad. The managers of the railroad thought that an African-American could not be a good engineer. McCoy accepted a less important job taking care of trains.

McCoy kept the trains' steam engines working *properly*. He also oiled the moving parts of the train. This had to be done while the train was stopped, which was dangerous. When trains were stopped for oiling, other trains sometimes ran into them. It took a lot of time to oil the trains. McCoy invented a device that could oil a train while

---

去学校上学。他对机械的工作原理非常感兴趣。他的父母把他送到了苏格兰的一所学校。在那学习，他成为了一名机械工程师。机械工程师设计机器。

当麦科伊在苏格兰时，美国内战爆发了。战争过后，他回到了家乡加拿大。很快地他去了密歇根并得到了一份铁路上的工作。铁路上的管理者认为一个美国黑人不可能是一个好的工程师。麦科伊得到了一份照看火车的不太重要的工作。

麦科伊使火车的蒸汽机正常工作。他也给正在行驶的火车加油。这应该是在火车停下来的时候才做的工作，他那样做是很危险的。有时当火车停下来加油时，其他的火车就会开进来。给火车加油会花很长时间。麦科伊发明一种可以给行进中的火车加油的设备。1872年，他获得了政府颁

---

civil war 内战　　　　　　　　　　　　properly *adv.* 正确地；适当地

it was moving. In 1872, he got a *patent* from the government to make and sell his *automatic* oil cup. A patent is a piece of paper that shows who came up with a particular idea or design.

In less than 10 years, the automatic oil cup was being used in trains, ships, and many kinds of steam engines. McCoy moved to Detroit in 1882. There he thought up ways to improve steam engines. He also invented a fold-up ironing board and an automatic *lawn sprinkler*. In 1920, he started his own business. He invented devices and sold them. He used the earnings to improve his inventions. McCoy liked to show his work to children in his neighborhood. He urged them to go to school. He hired young African-American men to work for him.

McCoy kept on inventing for the rest of his life. At the age of 80, he got a patent for a tire. In all, McCoy had 57 patents for his inventions.

发的一项专利，制造并出售他的自动加油杯。一项专利就是一份文件，它表明是谁提出的独特的想法或设计。

在不到十年内，自动加油杯被用在火车、轮船和许多种类的蒸汽机中。麦科伊在1882年去了底特律。在那他想出了改善蒸汽机的方法。他同时也发明了折叠熨衣板和自动草坪喷洒器。1920年，他开始了他自己的事业。他发明设备然后卖掉它们。用挣来的钱改进他的发明。麦科伊喜欢把他的工作展示给邻居的孩子们。他劝他们去上学。他雇用年轻的美国黑人为他工作。

在他的余生中麦科伊一直都在发明。在他80岁的时候他得到了一项轮胎的专利。至此，麦科伊的发明一共得到了57项专利。

---

patent *n.* 专利权；专利证书
lawn *n.* 草地；草坪

automatic *adj.* 自动的
sprinkler *n.* 洒水器；喷洒器

39

Why Do We Say That?

Have you ever heard someone say, "It's the real McCoy"? This means something is the best and not a *fake*. It is thought that this saying came from customers of Elijah McCoy. His device for oiling trains was so good that others tried to *duplicate* it. The railroads wanted McCoy's device and not a low-quality

我们为什么那样说?

你曾经听到有人说过"这是真的麦科伊"吗？这意味着这些东西是最好的而不是假的。这句话被认为来源于麦科伊的客户。他给火车加油的设备太好了以至于其他人想要复制它。铁路公司想要的是麦

---

fake *n.* 假货；赝品　　　　　　　　　　　　duplicate *v.* 复制

imitation. They wanted "the real McCoy."

Do you ever get so tired that you "run out of steam"? This *saying* comes from the steam engine. A steam engine has a fire that is made with coal. The fire boils water, which creates the steam that powers the engine. If a train uses up all of its coal, the water stops boiling and the engine runs out of steam. The train slows down and stops.

When you have to give someone bad news and you're not sure what to say, you might "beat around the bush." Rich hunters used to have their servants beat bushes and high grass to *drive out* the animals that were hiding there. If the servants beat around the outside of the bushes, the animals would often not come out.

科伊的设备而不是一件低质量的仿制品。他们想要"真正的麦科伊"。

你是否曾经感到很累以至于"耗尽了蒸汽"？这句话来源于蒸汽机。蒸汽机要由煤燃烧形成的火，火把水烧开而产生蒸汽为发动机提供动力。如果一列火车的煤全部用光了，水就停止加热了，蒸汽机的蒸汽也耗光了。火车就会减速而停下来。

当你想告诉某个人一个不好的消息又不确定说什么的时候，你可能会拐弯抹角。有经验的猎人会让他们的仆人拍打树丛和较高的草，然后将藏在其中的动物驱赶出来。如果仆人们拍打外边的灌木丛，动物通常不会出来。

---

imitation *n.* 仿制品；赝品
drive out 驱逐；驱散

saying *n.* 谚语；格言

Did you ever ask for a dozen doughnuts and get 13 instead? You got a "baker's dozen." In the Middle Ages, a person could be *punished* for selling less than he or she was paid for. Some bakers were not very good at counting. When they sold a dozen *loaves*, they gave out 13, just to be on the safe side.

你是否曾要求过要一打甜甜圈却得到13个？你得到的是面包师傅的一打。在中世纪的时候，一个人可能因为少卖给他或她所要买的东西而受到惩罚。一些面包师不是非常擅长数数。当他们卖一打面包时，他们给出去13个，仅仅在安全的边缘上。

---

punish *v.* 处罚；惩罚

loaf *n.* 一条面包

40

The Push and Pull of Magnets

There is an *invisible* force that can push and pull metal things. It sounds like magic, but it's real. This force is called *magnetism*.

People have known for many years that certain rocks have a pull on iron. These rocks contain *magnetite*, which is also called *lodestone*. Lodestone is a natural

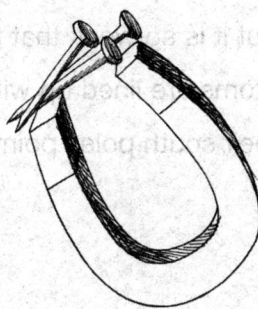

磁铁的斥力和引力

存在这样一种无形的力量可以吸引和排斥金属类的东西。这听起来很神奇，但这确实是真的。这种力量叫做磁力。

一直以来，人们就知道一些特定的岩石对铁有一种引力。这些岩石包含磁铁矿，磁铁矿也被叫做天然磁石。磁石是一种自然界中的磁体。

---

invisible *adj.* 看不见的；无形的   magnetism *n.* 磁性；磁力
magnetite *n.* 磁铁矿   lodestone *n.* 天然磁石

magnet.

Magnets are things that pull on some kinds of metal. This is why a magnet sticks to your *refrigerator*.

Everything is made up of tiny *particles* called *atoms*. Scientists think that each atom has a north pole and a south pole. These poles have opposite forces. In an object that is not a magnet, the atoms are not lined up in any particular way. The force of a north pole is balanced by the force of a nearby south pole. There may be a little magnetism, but it is so weak that the object won't attract metal. In a magnet, the atoms are lined up with all their north poles pointing one way and all their south poles pointing the other way. One end of the magnet now

---

磁铁是一种对某些金属有吸引力的物质。这就是为什么磁铁能固定在冰箱上。

每一种物质都是由一种叫做原子的微小粒子组成的。科学家认为每种原子都有南极和北极。它们是相反的力量。在没有磁性的物质中，原子不是按照特定的方式排列的。北极的磁力会被周围的南极的磁力平衡掉。也许这个物体会存在一点磁力，但是由于它太弱了而不能吸引金属。在磁体中，所有原子的排列都是北极指向一个方向，南极指向另一个方向。磁体

---

magnet *n.* 磁石；磁体   refrigerator *n.* 冰箱

particle *n.* 微粒；粒子   atom *n.* 原子

THE PUSH AND PULL OF MAGNETS

has the force of a north pole, while the other end has the force of a south pole.

A bar magnet is shaped like a long *rectangle*. The poles are at the ends of the bar. The opposite forces of the north and south poles attract each other. This pull from one end of the magnet to the other creates an area of force called a magnetic field. While north and south poles pull each other, two north poles or two south poles *repel*, or push away, each other. If you try to put the south poles of two magnets together, they will push each other apart.

Earth has magnetism. Picture Earth with a big bar magnet going through its center, with the North Pole at the top and the South Pole

---

的末端是北极的磁力，而另一端是南极的磁力。

一个磁棒的形状就像是一个长的矩形。磁极在磁棒的末端。北极和南极相反的磁力相互吸引。这种来自于磁铁一端对另一端的引力而形成的带力的区域叫做磁场。虽然北极和南极相互吸引，但是两个北极或两个南极相互排斥。如果你试着把两个磁体的南极放到一起，它们会互相排斥而分开。

地球有磁性。用一根通过地球中心的大的磁棒来描绘地球，北极在顶

---

rectangle *n.* 长方形；矩形 　　　　　　　　repel *v.* 排斥；相斥

123
MCGRAW-HILL

at the bottom. The magnetic north pole is near, but not exactly at, Earth's North Pole.

In a *compass*, the *needle* is a small magnet. The needle can turn freely. Its south pole is pulled toward Earth's magnetic north pole. The end of the needle that points north is sometimes red or marked with an N for "north."

Magnets have many other uses. Some construction *cranes* use them to lift heavy loads. Sound is recorded on magnetic tape. Many appliances have electric *motors*, which contain magnets.

部，南极在底部。磁铁的北极在地球的北极附近，但不是恰好在北极。

在罗盘中，指南针就是一个小的磁体。指南针可以自由旋转。它的南极会指向地磁北极。指南针的末端指向北极，有时是红色的或者标记上表示北极的字母N。

磁铁有许多其他的用途。一些建筑起重机会用磁铁来搬运重物。声音会被记录在磁带上。许多有发动机的家电都有磁铁。

---

compass *n.* 罗盘；指南针　　　　　　needle *n.* 指针
crane *n.* 起重机；吊车　　　　　　　motor *n.* 发动机；马达

41

The Senses

A sister and a brother are walking in the woods. She hears a bird singing and sees *raspberries* on long *thorny* stems. She avoids the thorns while picking a raspberry. It feels bumpy. She pops it into her mouth and says it tastes sweet. Her brother hears a *rustle* in the bushes and sees a snake *slither* out, so he moves away.

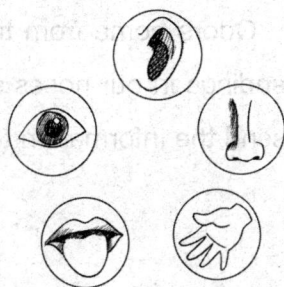

感觉

姐姐和弟弟正走在树林中。姐姐听到了鸟的叫声并且在一条很长的带刺的茎上发现了山莓。她避开了刺摘到了一个山莓。这有些困难。她把山莓扔进嘴里说它尝起来很甜。她的弟弟听到灌木丛中有沙沙声，然后看到了一条蛇在滑行，因此他离开了。

---

raspberry *n.* 山莓；树莓
rustle *n.* 轻轻的摩擦声；沙沙声

thorny *adj.* 有刺的；多刺的
slither *v.* 滑行；爬行

Our bodies have sense organs that collect outside information. Our brains use this information to decide how we should react. The five basic senses are sight, smell, taste, hearing, and touch.

Our eyes are sight organs. The dark center of the eye is the *pupil*. In bright light, the pupil grows smaller so that less light can get in. In the dark, the pupil grows bigger to let in more light. Behind the pupil is the *lens*, which bends the light and focuses it on the *retina*. There, special cells send the image to the brain.

Odors come from tiny particles that travel through the air. Nerve endings in our noses sense these particles, and the *olfactory* nerves send the information to the brain. This is how we smell a skunk or a

---

我们的身体有收集外界信息的感觉器官。我们的大脑利用这些信息决定我们应做什么反应。五个基本的感觉器官是视觉，嗅觉，味觉，听觉，触觉。

我们的眼睛是视觉器官，眼睛的黑色中心部分是瞳孔。在明亮的地方，瞳孔收缩，这样会进来较少的光。在黑暗中，瞳孔变大，更多的光可以进来。瞳孔的后面是晶状体，它把光折射聚焦到视网膜上。这样，特殊的细胞会把成像反映给大脑。

气味来自于空气中飘过的极其微小的颗粒。鼻子的神经末梢感觉到这些微粒，嗅觉神经就会把信息发送给大脑。这就是我们为什么会闻到臭鼬

---

pupil *n.* 瞳孔　　　　　　　　　　　　　　lens *n.* （眼球的）晶状体
retina *n.* 视网膜　　　　　　　　　　　　olfactory *adj.* 嗅觉的

plate of freshly baked cookies.

We taste substances with our tongues. Our tongues have special groups of cells called *taste buds*. The front of the tongue tastes sweet things, and the sides taste salty and sour things. The back of the tongue tastes bitter things. Our taste buds need *saliva* to work. The more we chew and mix saliva with the food, the better we taste it.

Our ears are shaped like cups to pick up sound waves. Inside the ear, a *canal* directs the sound to the *eardrum*. The sound waves vibrate the eardrum. Three small bones behind the eardrum pass the vibrations on to the inner ear. There, they are picked up by the auditory, or hearing nerve and carried to the brain.

或是一盘新烘烤出来的饼干。

我们用舌头来尝东西。我们的舌头由特殊的细胞组成，称为味觉细胞。舌头的前面是品尝甜的东西的，旁边是品尝咸的和酸的东西的。舌头的后面是尝苦的东西的。我们的味蕾需要唾液来工作。唾液和食物咀嚼混合的越充分，我们尝到的味道就越好。

我们耳朵的形状像杯子用来收集声波。在耳朵里，有一条管把声音和耳膜连在一起。声波使耳膜振动。耳膜后面的三块小骨把振动传到内耳。这样，它们通过听觉神经把声音传送到大脑中。

---

taste bud *n.* 味蕾
canal *n.* （人体内输送食物、空气等的）管；道

saliva *n.* 唾液
eardrum *n.* 耳膜；鼓膜

We use our sense of touch to feel our *surroundings*. Nerve endings in the skin send signals to the brain. We can feel temperature, roughness, and wetness. We can feel different shapes, and we can feel pain.

Besides the five basic senses, there are as many as fifteen other senses. We have sense organs deep inside our bodies that sense things such as our weight and body position. We have a sense of *balance*. We sense when we are hungry, thirsty, or tired.

我们用触觉器官感受我们周围的环境。皮肤的神经末梢把信号传递给大脑。我们能感觉到温度、粗糙度、湿润度。我们能感觉到不同的形状，感觉到疼痛。

除了这五个基本的感官，还有其他的十五种感官。在我们身体内部有感觉器官，可以感觉到体重或是身体的位置。我们有平衡感。当我们饥饿、口渴或疲劳时，我们可以感觉到。

---

surroundings *n.* 环境　　　　　　　　　　　　　balance *n.* 平衡；平衡能力

42

A Fish Out of Water

To do this science experiment, you will need *crayons*, two blank *index cards*, tape, and a pencil or wood *dowel* about 20 centimeters (8 inches) long.

Step one: Use the crayons to draw a fish in the middle of one index card. On the other card, draw a picture of a *fish tank*. The tank should be bigger than the fish.

不在水里的鱼

做这个实验需要彩色笔，两张空白的索引卡片，胶带，一支铅笔或是大约20厘米（8英寸）长的木头销子。

第一步：在一张索引卡的中间用彩色笔画一条鱼。在另外一张卡片上画一个鱼缸。鱼缸要比鱼大。

---

crayon *n.* 彩色铅笔（或粉笔、蜡笔）　　　　index card　索引卡
dowel *n.* 木钉；销子　　　　　　　　　　fish tank　鱼缸

Step two: Place the cards back to back. *Tape* them together along the sides, not along the top or bottom.

Step three: *Slide* the pencil or dowel between the cards. Tape the cards to the pencil so they are at the top of the pencil. The pencil should be in the center of the cards.

Step four: Hold the pencil between your *palms*. *Spin* the pencil while you look at the cards.

What happened? The fish looked as if it were in the tank. When your eyes send an image to your brain, it maintains the image for a short time. Your brain still saw the fish after it was gone. The same thing was true for the tank. The two images overlapped in your brain,

---

第二步：把两张卡片背对背放在一起。沿着边把它们用胶带粘起来，不要沿着顶部和底部。

第三步：让铅笔或木销在两张卡片之间滑动。把卡片用胶带固定在铅笔上，让它们在铅笔的上部。铅笔要在卡片的中心位置。

第四步：两个手握住铅笔，注视着卡片旋转铅笔。

发生了什么？鱼看起来好像在鱼缸里。当你的眼睛把这个画面传达到大脑中时，大脑会维持这个画面一小段时间。鱼消失之后，你的大脑仍然会看到它。鱼缸也是一样。两个画面在你的大脑中重叠，因此看上去好像

---

tape *v.* 用胶带粘贴　　　　　　　　　slide *v.* （使）滑行；滑动

palm *n.* 手掌；手心　　　　　　　　　spin *v.* （使）快速旋转

so it looked as if the fish were in the tank.

A filmed cartoon works in the same way. The *characters* seem to be moving. What you really see is a series of *still* pictures. In each one, the characters are in *slightly* different positions. When the pictures are shown quickly, one after another, the characters appear to move.

是鱼在鱼缸里。

动画片也是同样的工作原理。角色看起来好像在动。你真正看到的其实是一系列静止的图片。每一个图片里，角色都是在稍微不同的位置。当图片快速地一个接一个的演示时，角色就会动起来。

---

character *n.* 人物；角色　　　　　　　　　　still *adj.* 静止的
slightly *adv.* 略微；稍微

43

Telescopes and Microscopes

Scientists often use tools to help them learn about things. *Astronomers* are scientists who study stars, planets, and the rest of outer space. One tool that astromoners use is the *telescope*. Most telescopes are *optical*. This means that they work by collecting light from stars. An optical telescope focuses the light to form

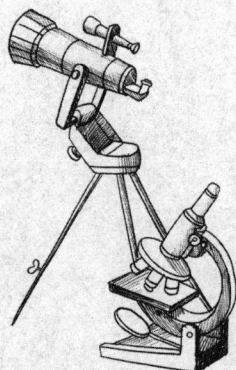

望远镜和显微镜

科学家们经常借助工具来研究事情。天文学家是研究恒星、行星和其他的外太空的科学家。天文学家使用的一种工具是望远镜。大多数的望远镜是光学的。这就意味着它们通过从星球上收集光来工

---

astronomer *n.* 天文学家
optical *adj.* 光学的

telescope *n.* 望远镜

an image. A *lens* at one end makes the image look larger.

Hans Lipperhey made one of the first telescopes. In 1608, he held one glass lens in front of another. When he looked through both, he found that objects looked much bigger.

Galileo was the first to use a telescope to look at the night sky. He saw that there were *craters* on the Moon. He studied the planets and figured out that they *revolve* around the Sun. Until then, people had thought that the Sun, the Moon, and the planets revolved around Earth.

The first telescopes worked by *refraction*. A glass lens was used to bend light to form an image. Light is made up of colors. A glass lens does not bend these colors evenly, so the image is not quite clear. In 1688, Isaac Newton made a reflecting telescope. It used mirrors to

---

作。光学望远镜把光聚焦而形成画面。末端的镜片会使画面看起来更大。

汉斯·李伯希制造了第一台望远镜。1608年，他把一个镜片放在了另一个镜片之前，当他通过两个镜片看东西时，他发现物体看起来更大。

伽利略是第一个在观察夜空时使用望远镜的人。他看到了月球上的陨石坑。他研究了行星并证实了它们围绕太阳运转。直到那时人们还认为太阳、月亮和其他的行星绕地球转。

第一台望远镜是通过光折射的现象来工作的。玻璃镜片可以使光发生折射而成像。光是由各种颜色组成的。玻璃镜片不能均匀地折射彩色光。因此，图像不是特别清晰。1688年，艾萨克·牛顿研制出了反射望

---

lens *n.* 透镜；镜片　　　　crater *n.* （由炸弹爆炸或巨物撞击形成的）坑

revolve *v.* 旋转；环绕　　　refraction *n.* 折射

make a clear image.

Now there are large telescopes in many places on Earth. They are used to help astronomers find new planets and to learn more about the universe. The Hubble Space Telescope orbits Earth. It sends back detailed pictures from space. Much of what we know about the universe has come from what people have seen through telescopes.

Microscopes are tools that scientists use to see very tiny things. We can see things through a microscope that we can't see with just our eyes.

A simple microscope has one lens and can *magnify* an object up to 15 times its normal size. *Compound microscopes* use two lenses. Some can magnify things up to 2,000 times their normal size. Many microscopes sit on a stand. You can look down through a *tube* that

---

远镜，它使用镜子，从而能够清晰地成像。

目前，地球上的很多地方都有大型望远镜。它们帮助天文学家找到新的行星，更深入的研究宇宙。哈伯太空望远镜绕地球运行。它从太空中发回详细的照片。我们了解的关于宇宙的大部分都是人们从望远镜中看到的。

显微镜是科学家观察非常微小的东西的工具。我们可以通过显微镜来观察肉眼看不到的东西。

一个简单的显微镜有一个镜片，可以把物体放大到正常的15倍。复合显微镜有两个镜片。一些能把物体放大到正常的两千倍。许多显微镜固

---

microscope *n.* 显微镜
compound microscope 复显微镜

magnify *v.* 放大
tube *n.* 管；管子

MCGRAW-HILL

contains the lenses. At the bottom is a stage that holds the object you want to see. A light enables you to see the stage. To focus on the object, you can move the lens closer to or farther from the object.

The most powerful microscope is the *electron* microscope, which is used for looking at cells. It can magnify an object to about 250,000 times its normal size.

定在一个座上。你可以通过一个包含镜片的管观察。在底部是一个平台，在上边可以放你想要观察的物体。有光可以让你看到平台。为了集中观察物体，你可以把镜片靠近或远离所观察的物体。

最有效的显微镜是电子显微镜，它是用来观察细胞的。它可以把物体放大到正常的250 000倍。

electron *n.* 电子

44

An Important Scientist

Robert Hooke was a scientist who lived in the 1600s. Hooke made the first compound microscope. He observed thin slices of *cork*. Cork is the light outer bark of a tree. Hooke saw that the cork had tiny holes, or *pores*, that were irregular in size and shape. They reminded him of a *honeycomb*. He used the word cells to

一位重要的科学家

罗伯特·胡克是一位生活在17世纪的科学家。胡克研制出了第一台复合显微镜。他用显微镜观察软木薄片。软木是树皮外部质地轻的部分。他发现软木有小洞或气孔。它们的形状和大小都不规则，这使他想到了蜂巢。他用细胞这个词描绘他所看到的。胡克是第一个看到植

---

cork *n.* 软木；木栓
honeycomb *n.* 蜂巢

pore *n.* 孔隙；气孔

describe what he saw. Hooke was the first person to see plant cells. Some of the other things that Hooke saw under the microscope were bird feathers, *sponges*, and insects. He wrote about what he saw and made detailed drawings. These went into his book Micrographia.

Hooke was also the first person to look at *fossils* with a microscope. Some scientists of the time thought that fossils were just stones with unusual patterns. Hooke looked at *petrified* wood, which is wood that has turned into stone. He compared it with rotten wood. He described how water that had minerals could turn dead wood to stone. He also looked at fossils under his microscope. Some fossils did not look like any living thing on Earth. Hooke

---

物细胞的人。他在显微镜下看到的其他东西还有羽毛，海绵和昆虫等。他记录并详细画出了他所看到的。这些都写入了他的《显微图谱》一书中。

胡克也是第一个用显微镜观察化石的人。一些科学家认为化石只是有着不同图案的石头。他观察石化的木头，也就是木头变成的石头。与腐木相比较，他描述了水中的矿物质是如何把木头变成石头的。他也在他的显

---

sponge *n.* 海绵
petrified *adj.* 石化的

fossil *n.* 化石

figured out that some fossils were from *extinct* species.

Hooke also built a telescope and observed the planets. He studied earthquakes. He drew maps and designed buildings. He was famous for his work on clocks and watches. It is amazing that one person could make so many important discoveries in so many areas of science.

微镜下观察化石。一些化石看起来不像任何地球上的生物。胡克指出有些化石是来自绝迹的物种。

胡克还制造出了观察行星的望远镜。他研究地震。他画地图，设计建筑。他以在时针和手表方面的影响而著称。一个人能在这么多科学领域有这么多重要的发现是一件不可思议的事。

extinct *adj.* 已灭绝的；绝种的

45

The Life Cycle of a Tree

A tree begins to grow when it *sprouts* from a seed. The seed comes from a parent tree. There are two ways that trees make seeds. Trees that make seeds from flowers are angiosperms. When the flowers are pollinated, they produce seeds that are protected by coverings called fruits.

Not all of these trees have the kind of

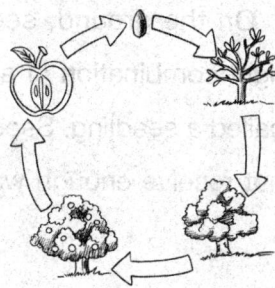

树的年轮

种 子萌芽后树木开始生长。种子来自于母树。树产生种子有两种方式。从花中得到种子的树木是被子植物。当花被授粉后，产生种子，种子被果实包裹着。

并不是所有的树木都能结出你在商店所能买到的果实。例如，柳树的

---

sprout *v.* 发芽；抽芽

fruit you buy at the store. For example, the *willow* tree has a fruit you would not want to eat. Its fruit is a dry *capsule-shaped* object that bursts open and releases seeds. Willow seeds have fluffy fibers that float in the wind. They can float a long way before landing. Some trees' seeds are carried to new locations by water or animals.

Trees that do not reproduce by growing flowers are called *gymnosperms*. Gymnosperms have cones that form seeds when they are pollinated. The seeds fall from the cones to the ground.

On the ground, seeds *germinate*, or sprout, when they get the right combination of air, water, and sun. The tiny stem that grows is called a seedling. Seedlings may die if the soil is moved or if they do not receive enough water. A seedling that grows to a height of 180

果实你就不会想吃。柳树的果实是一种胶囊形的物体，它会裂开并释放出种子。柳树的种子有柳絮飘在空中。它们在落地之前会飘过很长时间。一些树的种子被水或动物等送到新的地方。

不是由生长的花产生种子的植物叫裸子植物。当裸子植物授粉时，它的球果会形成种子。种子从球果中脱落掉在地上。

在地面上，当种子获得合适的空气、水和阳光之后，它们发芽生长。长出的细小的茎称为幼苗。如果土壤被换或幼苗没有得到充足的水分时，

---

willow *n.* 柳；柳树　　　　　　capsule-shaped *adj.* 具有（或呈）胶囊形状的
gymnosperm *n.* 裸子植物　　　　germinate *v.* （使）发芽；开始生长

centimeters (6 feet) is called a *sapling*.

As trees grow taller, their trunks get larger, and they grow new branches. This growth is caused by a group of special cells called the *cambium* at the inner surface of the *bark*. These cells divide to make *xylem* cells near the center of the trunk and phloem cells near the bark. Xylem cells carry water, and phloem cells carry food. As the roots grow, they take up more and more water and nutrients from the soil.

The leaves produce food for the tree through a process called photosynthesis. The tree uses the food for energy to live and grow. Leaves give off water into the air. If this water is not replaced, the leaves wilt. Water from the roots is pulled up to the leaves by the

---

幼苗就会死亡。幼苗长到180厘米（6英尺）时叫做树苗。

树长得越高，它们的树干就会变得越大，并且会长出新的分枝。这种生长是由树皮表面内部叫做形成层的一种特殊细胞引起的。这些细胞分裂为树干中心附近的木质部的细胞和树皮附近韧皮部的细胞。木质部细胞运送水，韧皮部细胞运输养料。由于根的生长，它们会从土壤中吸收越来越多的水和营养。

叶子通过一种叫做光合作用的过程来为树木生产养料。树木利用养料生存和生长。叶子向空气中释放水分。如果水分不能循环，叶子就会枯

---

sapling *n.* 幼树
bark *n.* 树皮

cambium *n.* 形成层；新生组织
xylem *n.* 木质部

xylem.

Trees grow faster when there are more nutrients and water than when the soil is poor or dry. If you cut a tree *trunk* and look at the wood, you will see rings. Each ring was formed during one growth season. Wide rings form when conditions are good. A thin ring means it was a poor year for growth.

萎。根部的水通过木质部运输到叶子里。

　　当土壤中有更多的营养物质和水时树木要比土壤贫瘠或干燥时生长得快。如果你砍掉一个树干看看，你会发现上面有年轮。每一个生长季节形成一圈。当生长条件好时会形成宽的年轮。窄的年轮意味着这一年的生长条件不佳。

---

trunk *n.* 树干

46

Growing Applesauce

One morning, Mom looked out the kitchen window and said, "I wish we had an apple tree in the backyard." My sister and I agreed, so we went to a plant *nursery*. There we chose an apple tree that was about the same height as my mom. The tree was growing out of a big ball of *dirt wrapped* in *burlap*. We also bought a big

"长出来"的苹果酱

　　一天早晨，妈妈透过厨房窗户向外看，说道："我希望能在后院种一棵苹果树"。姐姐和我都赞同，所以我们去了一家植物苗圃。在那里，我们挑选了一棵和我母亲一样高的苹果树。苹果树是在一个大的泥土球中长出来的，这个泥土球是用粗麻布包裹起来的。我们也买了

---

nursery *n.* 花圃　　　　　　　　dirt *n.* 泥土；散土
wrap *v.* 包；裹　　　　　　　　burlap *n.* 粗麻布；打包麻布

bag of *peat moss*, which looked like black soil.

At home, Mom used the *wheelbarrow* to push the tree to the backyard. I carried the peat moss. My sister brought the shovel.

In the backyard, Mom handed me the shovel, pointed to the ground, and said, "Dig." I dug. Mom said the hole had to be as deep as the burlap ball.

When the hole was deep enough, Mom poured in the peat moss, and I mixed it into the dirt with the shovel. The peat moss made the soil more *conducive* to tree growth.

My sister and I rolled the tree into the hole. Then we removed the plastic string that was *wound* around the burlap, but we left the

---

一大包泥煤苔，它看上去像黑色的土壤。

在家里，妈妈用独轮车把树推到后院，我搬运泥煤苔。我姐姐拿铲子。

在后院，妈妈把铲子给我，指着地面说："挖坑。"然后我就开始挖坑。妈妈说这个坑应该和泥煤苔的高度一样深。

当坑足够深的时候，妈妈向里面倾倒泥煤苔，我用铲子将它混合进泥土中。泥煤苔使土壤更加有助于树的生长。

我姐姐和我把树移到坑里。然后我们把粗麻布周围损坏的塑料绳子拿

---

peat moss 泥煤苔
conducive *adj.* 有助（于…）的

wheelbarrow *n.* 独轮车；手推车
wind *v.* 缠绕；绕成团

burlap. "The roots will grow right through it," Mom explained. Next, we shoveled dirt into the hole, about halfway up the ball. Then Mom brought the *hose* and filled the hole with water. When the water disappeared, we finished filling the hole with dirt.

As we admired our apple tree, Mom said, "*Applesauce* in about five years."

掉。但是我们留下了粗麻布。"有它根会很好的生长，"妈妈解释说。接下来，我们用铲子把泥土填进坑中，大约填到泥土球一半的位置。妈妈拿来一根塑料水管，把坑填满水。当水消失之后，我们用土把坑填满。

当我们夸我们的苹果树的时候，妈妈说："大约五年之后我们能吃到苹果酱了。"

---

hose *n.* （灭火，浇花等用的）橡皮软管；塑料软管　　　　applesauce *n.* 苹果酱

47

How Animals Defend Themselves

Animals that live in the wild must protect themselves from becoming meals for other animals. One way is to hide. *Prairie dogs* are rodents that live in "towns" made up of many burrows, underground holes used for *shelter*. If any prairie dog sees a threat, such as a *hawk*, it sounds a warning cry. The others pick up this cry,

动物们怎样保护自己

生活在野外的动物必须要保护它们自己不变成其他动物的食物。一种方法是隐蔽。土拨鼠是啮齿类动物，它们住在由许多地洞组成的"城镇"中，这些地下的洞是它们的藏身处。如果任何一个土拨鼠发现威胁，例如鹰，它就会发出警告声。其他的土拨鼠听到这个声音，它

---

prairie dog 土拨鼠　　　　　　　　　　　shelter *n.* 遮蔽；庇护
hawk *n.* 鹰

and all the prairie dogs hide in their burrows.

Another way some animals hide is by blending in with the background. This trick is called *camouflage*. The rose thorn hopper is a bug that looks like a thorn. It sits very still on a rose bush and faces the same way as the actual thorns. *Arctic* hares have white fur during the winter. They look like the snow that is all around them. When the snow melts, their fur changes to a *speckled* gray.

Some animals make themselves look big to scare away enemies. *Puffer fish* use water or air to blow themselves into a large ball. They also have spines, which make the ball seem more threatening. Cheetah cubs have long manes until they are three months old. The manes make them look bigger than they are.

Other animals protect themselves by being fast. A pronghorn

们就会藏在它们的洞里。

另外一种方式是一些动物通过和周围的环境相混淆来隐藏自己。这一招叫做伪装。玫瑰刺跳虫是一种看起来像玫瑰刺的昆虫，它待在玫瑰丛中，像真的刺一样朝向。北极的野兔在冬天的时候是白色的毛。它们看上去像周围的雪一样。当雪融化了，它们的毛就会变成有斑点的灰色。

一些动物使它们自己看起来强大而吓走敌人。河豚鱼利用水或空气把自己吹成一个大球。它们也有刺，这会使这个球看上去更有威胁性。猎豹幼崽在长到三个月大之前会有很长的鬃毛。这些鬃毛使它们看上去比实际大。

其他的动物通过变快来保护自己。叉角羚羊奔跑的速度可以达到每小

---

camouflage *n.* （动物的）保护色；保护形状
speckled *adj.* 布满斑点的

arctic *adj.* 北极的
puffer fish 河豚鱼

antelope can run up to 90 kilometers per hour (55 miles per hour). Some lizards can run up to 30 kilometers per hour (19 miles per hour).

When an opossum is afraid, it plays dead. Other animals are good actors. If a person gets too close to a *killdeer*'s nest, the mother bird makes a lot of noise and *flaps* its wings as if it is hurt. Then it tries to lead the person away from the nest.

A skunk does not hide or run but *sprays* an oil that smells terrible. Skunks are not the only ones to use scent as a defense; *mink*, snakes, and foxes do too.

Some animals have tough outer coverings. Armadillos have hard plates on their back and sides. When under attack, they curl up to protect their soft bellies. Many tortoises have strong shells.

时90千米(每小时55英里)。一些蜥蜴速度能达到每小时30千米(每小时19英里)。

当一些负鼠害怕时，它们会装死。另一些动物是很好的演员。如果一个人离喧鸻的巢很近的时候，鸟妈妈会制造一些噪声并且拍动翅膀，就好像它受伤了一样。然后它会试图让人远离它的巢。

臭鼬既不隐藏也不逃跑，而是释放一种很难闻的气体。臭鼬不是唯一使用气味来抵御敌人的动物；貂、蛇和狐狸也是如此。

一些动物有坚硬的外壳。在犰狳的背上和侧面有坚硬的壳。当它们面临攻击时，它们会卷曲起来保护它们柔软的肚子。许多龟类有很硬的外壳。

---

killdeer *n.* 喧鸻；小水鸟   flap *v.* 拍打；拍击

spray *v.* 喷；喷洒   mink *n.* 水貂；貂

Many animals fight to defend themselves. Sometimes they must fight members of their own species over *territory*. Bears and owls *scratch* with their claws. Some sheep and goats attack with their horns. *Ostriches* and kangaroos kick with their legs. Mice, squirrels, and wolves bite with their teeth.

许多动物为了保护自己而战斗。有时候，它们为了领地必须和与自己同种族的成员战斗。熊和猫头鹰用它们的爪子去抓。一些羊用角去攻击。鸵鸟和袋鼠用腿踢。小鼠、松鼠和狼会用它们的牙咬。

---

territory *n.* 领地；管区　　　　　　　　　　scratch *v.* 划破；抓破
ostrich *n.* 鸵鸟

48

Animals Keeping Clean

When people are dirty, they take a bath or a shower. Animals don't have bars of soap or bathtubs, but they do keep themselves clean. Many furry animals, such as dogs and cats, keep themselves clean by *licking* their fur. They also use their teeth to bite fleas and *ticks* or to pull out small *clumps* of dirt. Cats have rough

动物保持干净

当人们脏了的时候，他们会洗澡或淋浴。动物没有洗澡用的香皂或浴盆，但是它们仍然会让自己保持干净。许多毛绒绒的动物，比如狗和猫，它们通过舔自己的皮毛让自己保持干净。它们也用牙齿去咬跳蚤和蜱虫或者是扒出小块的脏东西。猫的舌头很粗糙。它们在舔自

lick *v.* 舔
clump *n.* 堆；缕

tick *n.* 扁虱；蜱

tongues. When they lick their fur, it is almost as if they are being combed with a wet *bristle* brush.

Some animals that live in groups clean each other. Chimpanzees often *groom* one another. One chimp may groom an area that the other chimp can't reach.

Birds take baths to stay clean. First they wade in shallow water. Next they beat their wings. Then they fluff out their feathers to dry. Birds also take dust baths on the ground. It is thought that they do this to rid themselves of *pests* such as *lice*.

Even fish need cleaning. Fish have tiny animals called parasites that live on their scales and in their mouths. Parasites use other animals' bodies for sustenance. Some fish and shrimp live by eating these pests off other fish. Such fish are called "cleaner fish." Larger

---

己的毛的时候，几乎就像是用一把湿的刚毛刷子在梳理毛发。

一些群居的动物会相互清洁。黑猩猩经常为另一个黑猩猩梳理毛发。一个黑猩猩会为另一个梳理它够不到的地方。

鸟类通过洗澡保持干净。首先它们在浅水中涉水。然后它们会拍打翅膀，抖开羽毛。这样它们的羽毛就会干了。鸟类也会在陆地上用灰尘洗澡。它们这样做可能是在去除自身的虫害，比如虱子。

鱼甚至也需要清洁。鱼鳞上和鱼嘴中存在许多微小的被叫做寄生虫的生物。寄生虫通过其他动物的身体来获取营养。一些鱼和虾通过吃其他的

---

bristle *n.* 短而硬的毛发；刚毛
pest *n.* 害虫；害兽

groom *v.* 理毛；梳毛
louse *n.* 虱；虱子

fish will open their mouths wide so that the cleaner fish can get in to clean.

Sometimes, one kind of animal cleans another kind. One example is the tick bird. It eats ticks from the backs of *rhinoceroses*.

鱼类身上的害虫生存。这些鱼被叫做"清洁工鱼"。大鱼都会把嘴张大让清洁工鱼进来清理。

有时，一种动物会为另一种动物清洗。一个例子就是蜱虫鸟。它吃犀牛背上的蜱虫。

---

rhinoceros *n.* 犀牛